MY REHAB
IS SPELLED
J-E-S-U-S

*A book of hope for those
who may have a loved one
locked in an addiction*

KIM BARLOW

Trilogy Christian Publishers
A Wholly Owned Subsidiary of Trinity Broadcasting Network
2442 Michelle Drive
Tustin, CA 92780

For information, address Trilogy Christian Publishing
Rights Department, 2442 Michelle Drive, Tustin, Ca 92780.
Trilogy Christian Publishing/ TBN and colophon are trademarks of Trinity Broadcasting Network.

For information about special discounts for bulk purchases, please contact Trilogy Christian Publishing.

Manufactured in the United States of America

10 9 8 7 6 5 4 3 2 1

Library of Congress Cataloging-in-Publication Data is available.

ISBN 978-1-64773-017-8 (Print Book)
ISBN 978-1-64773-018-5 (ebook)

Dedication

I dedicate this book to my daughter, Dawn, who, through it all, has taught me the true meaning of love and forgiveness. She is the most courageous woman I know.

Contents

Foreword

Kim Barlow's true-life story is the kind of story that proves that Christ can save anyone, anywhere, at any time, making it the type of testimony that makes me want to praise the Lord!

I pray that it will help others find God's grace and truth for their own life.

—Rev. Travis A. Bennett, Senior Pastor
Saint Stephen United Methodist Church, Amarillo, Tx

How in the world does a man with a one-hundred-dollar-a-day, eighteen-year addiction to meth, a failed marriage and a ruined life, find a new entity that's clean, sober, and successful?

There is only one way: A Man comes from another world, enters our society, and takes our addiction upon the Cross, all while giving a new life to replace the old.

Kim Barlow's book, *My Rehab Is Spelled J-E-S-U-S*, is not so much about Kim Barlow as it is Jesus Christ! Jesus is the Chain-breaker, the Difference-maker, and the Life-giver.

Because of Jesus, Kim is just one of many thousands now "High On Hope." I am honored and thrilled to recommend his new book.

—Stan Cosby, former Senior Pastor
Saint Stephen United Methodist Church,
Amarillo, TX, and currently Senior Pastor of
Hedly, TX, United Methodist Church

I have been blessed to hear Kim's testimony a number of times. Each time I am reminded of how God works in miraculous ways. He brings hope to the hopeless, strength to the weak. From dealing meth to sharing the hope of Christ, Kim shows how God works through his life. For those that have or are fighting addiction or just needing some hope, this testimony is a must. J-e-s-u-s changes everything.

—Pastor Matt Johnson, Loft Church, Amarillo, Tx

Love changes people. God is that one Love, and seeing Kim's life journey, he will reveal how anyone can overcome and become a new person in Jesus Christ.

—David Hudson, Amarillo, Tx

Acknowledgments

Certain people have significantly influenced me in my walk called life. I look up to my parents, Stu, and Alice on how to raise four boys as the most positive role models. Our parents taught us respect for others as well as integrity before God. Mom and Dad worked long hours, yet weren't too tired to get four boys up and ready for church every Sunday. Because of their great faith in God, I know now what they instilled in me as a young boy, has made me who I am today.

My goal in writing this book is if I can help one person away from the devil's drug called meth then, my goal is complete.

I want to thank my brother Larry who never gave up on me. I must have been thirteen or fourteen years old when Larry invited me to the church he attended. The pastor gave an altar call, and something tugged for me to go on stage, where I accepted Jesus into my heart.

And thank you, Deborah Elliott-Upton, for encouraging me and coaching me to write this book. Without her, this never would have been possible.

Foremost, I want to thank my precious Savior, Jesus Christ, for His amazing grace to bring me out of an eighteen-year addiction to meth with no traditional rehab.

My salvation was just another miracle. Therefore, I articulate, "My Rehab Is Spelled J-e-s-u-s."

Chapter 1

Around 2:00 AM on Saturday, my phone rang. Sometimes I stayed awake for three days in a row, high on meth. Who would be calling me at this time of day? It wasn't unusual for me to be up so early, but the phone startled me.

I had rules for all my buyers—no calls after 10:00 PM. Doing business late at night or pre-sunrise was an invitation to get caught. Police training includes watching for such incidents. Usually, people out in the early mornings are up to no good. Me meeting someone to either buy or sell drugs created a suspicious activity to police officers.

Caller ID stated the call was from one of my regular buyers, Joe. As I answered, Joe, blurted, "Barlow, I'm desperate, and I need to purchase some *stuff* right now!"

We often called meth *stuff.* The problem with this scenario? I was out of meth myself and was waiting on my dealer to supply me. Being without a supply was never a good time. When my amount was out, I started to get anxious because I didn't have any meth either for me to sell or consume.

"Sorry, man, I don't have any right now, and I'm waiting on my guy to call me," I answered back.

Joe yelled into his phone, "You're a liar, Barlow. I don't believe you, and I am on my way to your house."

His tone revealed his anger as he ranted like a crazed man, not stopping to hear my answer. I recognized the desperation coming from him, but I had never heard him sound this inconsolable.

Fearful, I replied, "Joe, why would I lie to you? I don't have any right now. You and I have known each other for a long time. You know I wouldn't lie to you, man! Please calm down."

Joe's voice ramped up louder. He sounded out of his mind. He took maybe twenty seconds between words before he answered like Joe was having to try and think before he could talk. His frustration level increased as he struggled for responses—and those were making less and less sense. It seemed like I was reasoning with a cranky toddler.

I wondered if I behaved the same when I was desperate for a hit.

He screamed, *You better be ready, Barlow, because you're a damn liar. I'm coming to your house, and I'm going to kill you when I get there!*

I *was* out of meth. I was in need too. It had been a few hours since I had consumed, and the effects of no meth were setting in on me also. Being without meth makes it hard to keep eyes open. The experience of feeling sleepy simultaneously, all the mind can think about is getting that next hit to function.

In desperation, being without made me start to get the used bags, my meth came in from my dealer to see if I had left maybe one little spec in those baggies. Sometimes I would lick the inside getting any residue left. The taste was so bitter I would gag.

The more I repeated I was out, the more Joe screamed "I'm on my way, and you better be ready."

Because I couldn't convince him I was being honest or get him to calm down, my anxiety was rising.

With each passing second, my hands grew more sweaty. My heart was pounding. I warned my girlfriend at the time, "If he kicks the front door down, go hide in the closet." We were both frightened, wondering what Joe's next steps would be.

Joe was a large burly man and towered over me. His bulk and stature almost doubled me in size. His demeanor alone announced he had been around the block a time or two and probably enjoyed fighting for fighting's sake. My mind challenged me. What should I do next?

I considered my neighbors in the early morning hours of this morning. They would undoubtedly hear yelling and the banging if Joe tried to kick in my door. Would they call the police? I did not want the police around my house. This situation screamed of a drug deal going bad.

I could have easily called the police myself to intercept someone threatening to kill me. What would I say if I did: *Yes, police? I have a customer coming to kill me because I am out of meth, and he is on his way saying he was going to kill me when he got here!*

Besides, I didn't want them inside my house because of all the paraphernalia I had scattered inside my home.

All my thoughts suggested my entrapment due to my addiction once again. Times like these, I started to wonder how I could have got involved in the drug culture in the first place.

Reality kicked in like a hammer coming down on my head. What would happen if Joe broke through my door? Was this my day to die? All I could do was wait.

When Joe finally hung up, my hands were shaking uncontrollably. My adrenaline increased as my will for existence pressed on me.

Joe wasn't joking. He called every three or four minutes delivering a warning, he was on his way to my house and would kill me if I didn't give him the dope he needed. Like GPS, Joe announced his new location with each call. He was edging closer and closer.

At this moment, I wished my dealer would give me the call telling me he had a supply for me. Not just to appease Joe, but to free me from my torture, too. A call from my dealer would be most welcome right now.

I didn't want to die. Survival mode kicked in like the meth, quickly and without hesitation. Discerning Joe was getting closer; I retrieved my twelve-gauge pump shotgun from the bedroom closet. I opened my credenza next to my bed, where I stored my shells. I loaded five rounds into the gun, pushing them into the magazine. The first pump of a shotgun is a hair-raising sound. I grabbed the wooden stock connected to the twenty-eight-inch barrel, pulling it down and back up. The familiar sound, "shick-shick," deposits the first shell in the chamber ready to fire. Anyone who hears the sound of a shotgun pumping the first round into the firing mechanism knows this means caution.

I returned to the living room, ready to protect myself from this man I had considered a friend and possibly my new enemy. I sat at my desk at about twenty feet from the front door. Struggling to stay awake, I trembled with fear by preparing what I was to do before daybreak.

My girlfriend kept asking me if I was going to shoot Joe if he entered through my front door by kicking it down? I assured her if he went that far, I was going to protect us from him killing us.

I leaned the gun standing next to me at my computer desk, keeping one hand on the barrel. I waited for what seemed like an eternity.

Each passing minute seemed like an hour. Sadly, I wasn't thinking twice about getting ready to kill a man, nor reasoning how it would ruin my life forever.

The time that passed waiting on, Joe gave me time to think about what I would do when he arrived. This man was undoubtedly capable of kicking my door down.

I made up my mind. With clenched teeth, if Joe broke in, the only choice I had was to protect my girlfriend and me. I squared my shoulders and prepared to shoot him. What I'd do after, I had no idea.

A shotgun broadcasts a large number of pellets over a full pattern. Unlike a pistol shooting one bullet in a straight line, the farther away the target is from the barrel of a shotgun, the wider the pellets fan out.

The sound would be deafening inside the enclosed room. I had hunted with this gun before, so I knew the bang it imparted outdoors. I'd felt the powerful recoil each time as it fired a shell.

As I waited, I kept visualized Joe bounding through the door, coming toward me like a raging lion ready to attack its prey. My hope was he would see the shotgun, hear the sound of "shick-shick" of a shell pumping in, being enough for him to turn around and leave. If not, I prepared to shoot this man—my friend. A violent movie scene of a drug deal gone bad sped through my mind.

I waited. Every moment etched into my memory was worse than the last. Joe was coming, and he was coming for me. I can't begin to imagine how the guilt of this early morning could ruin my life forever. The impact on not only my family but Joe's family too would destroy both of us.

Chapter 2

As I waited for Joe, my thoughts repeatedly returned to my family. I am the youngest of four boys. My eldest brother, Scotty, is a decade older than me. The second-born, Randy, was born two years following Scotty. Larry was Mom and Dad's third son two years later. Almost six and one-half years exist between Larry, the third born, and me.

Our parents saw to it we were raised in a beautiful Christian home. Being the baby of the family, they spoiled me to an extent. I was a decent kid, not getting into much mischief or trouble. Even in the right Christian family, a person can be tempted by the evil one. However, through God's undeserving grace, He can and will save a sinner like me.

In my adult life, I have often wondered how my parents instilled so much respect for them from my brothers and me. I know it wasn't the fear of the paddle or spankings because one swat on my butt is my only memory of the discipline I ever received. Both of my parents had that look on their faces when I knew I was acting out, causing me to stop in my tracks.

Once when I was nine years old, my mother wouldn't let me do something I wanted to do. Today I can't recall what was so important to me at the time. When she said, "No," I walked away from her stomping my feet simply because she told me, "No."

Our back-door had a center pane of glass. When I stormed out, I slammed the door so hard, the glass shattered. My mom hurried toward the sound of the breaking glass to see what had happened, but more so to find out if I was okay.

I recollect I never intended to slam the door so hard. All I wanted to do was show my disapproval. All afternoon I worried because my mom told me she'd let Daddy handle this. I worried about my dad's reaction.

When Daddy came home from work, I wanted to hide. Instead, I informed him I had broken the garage door window. Daddy informed me Mother has already told him about it. Daddy and I proceeded to the garage door. As we looked at the broken glass, Daddy turned to me and said, "Kim, don't ever do this again."

Though Daddy didn't physically punish me, his loving attitude expressed more than any punishment could have done. I felt ashamed of what I had done.

Despite our parents' love, my brothers weren't perfect, either. I never wished to get in trouble like my older brothers occasionally did.

My brother Randy, during his last year of junior high school, became involved with the "wrong crowd" and associated with some thugs at school. Randy had been on the A-B Honor Roll through the ninth grade.

Everything changed when he befriended these not-so-nice young men. Receiving his driver's license seemed to be when his rebellion began.

My parents owned a clothing store, and at least twice a year, traveled five hours to the clothing market in Dallas to purchase new clothing for the store.

At eight or nine years old, my parents left me with my three older brothers while they traveled to Market, leaving mid-week and returning on Sunday evening. My parents, of course, thought I was in good hands, leaving me with my older siblings.

Saturday evening, Randy had invited several of his new friends to our house. Someone brought beer, and the party was on.

Around midnight, Randy and a couple of his pals, Tim and David, decided they wanted to go to a local park and drive around. The park was a popular place for kids to meet. Randy didn't want to leave me at the house by myself, so we all loaded into his car and drove to the park. Randy and David sat in front while Tim and I shared the backseat.

Randy's slurred speech indicated to me he had too much alcohol to be driving. But being my older brother, I perceived he knew what he was doing.

Arriving at the park, we were circling the hang-out spot when David yelled out, "Randy, look out!" A loud boom followed by scraping of metal to metal as Randy side-swiped a car parked on the street. I laid down in the back-floor board to hide.

When my brother hit the parked car, he must have been even more scared than me. In his drunkenness, he decided to drive home hurriedly. As the car sped around corners, the tires screeched. I hunkered down on the back floorboard. By the grace of God, we made it home safe, and Randy not being caught. I wonder now how he explained to my parents the damage to the side of his car.

Many times, I witnessed Randy giving my parents grief. Watching his rebellion and how it affected my parents taught me I never wanted them to deal with anything wrong because of my actions and my respect for them.

If anything were going to send me down the wrong path, it would have been me watching Randy as I was growing up. Randy's entire life seemed like he was spinning out of control. He was addicted to alcohol, cocaine, and even times of crack during his adult life and the time before the Lord turned his life around.

One morning, sometime after midnight in May of 1998, Randy had gone to a crack dealers' home to buy some crack. When he entered the house, three large men came out from another part of the house, now entering the room where Randy and his contact were.

Recounting the story to me, Randy said one of the men approached him, asking how much money Randy had. When Randy told them he only had fifty dollars to purchase his crack, the man called my brother a liar and started toward him.

When the man was close enough to Randy, the man grabbed him and tackled him to the floor. The two other men joined in to hold Randy down. They began hitting, kicking, and beating my brother severely. These three men overpowered him. All he could do was take his beating.

Randy believed these were going to be some of his last breaths on earth. Though the pain was excruciating, Randy found the men were beating him so hard; he became numb to the pain. The neighbors heard the commotion coming from the house and called the police about the disturbance.

While severely beaten, these men went through Randy's pockets, keeping his wallet and the fifty dollars. Critically injured, bleeding profusely, and going in and out of consciousness, the men dragged Randy to his car. They intended to drive him to the country, steal his car, and dump him in the bushes to die.

While opening the trunk to stuff him in, a police car sped toward them. When the gang saw the police car, they ran into the early morning dark neighborhood's recesses and disappeared.

Around 1:00 AM, I was startled out of a sound sleep by the phone's ringing. Caller ID indicated it was one of our local hospital's calling. A lady calling from the emergency room asked if Randy was my brother?

Still foggy from a sound sleep, I answered, "Randy is my brother. Is there something wrong with him?"

The lady on the phone said you need to come to the hospital; *your brother is in critical condition.*

Dressing quickly, I hurried to the hospital. At the reception desk, I stated who I was, and inquired about my brother. She motioned for me to come to the two closed doors leading to the emergency rooms.

Meeting me at the doors, she opened them, "Follow me," she said. As we proceeded down the long hall, the lights made it seem like daytime though it was pitch black outside. Coming to the end of the hallway, she pointed into the room, saying, "There's your brother."

He was reclining in his hospital bed, and I hardly recognized Randy due to the beating he had received earlier. Looking at his head, it swelled so badly; Randy could barely see through his swollen and bruised eyes. Dried blood caked almost everywhere my eyes could see.

Randy asked me to look at his body beneath his hospital gown. All I could see was severe bruising from his head to his toes. They had beaten him to the point I couldn't see anything but black-and-blue marks all over his body.

The ER doctor informed me Randy's orbit around his eyes shattered in his face, a broken jaw, broken collarbone, broken scapula, and several ribs were part of their diagnosis. He received two-hundred and forty-five stitches that early morning.

The doctor noted Randy's condition was life-threatening due to bleeding inside his skull. The next twenty-four to forty-eight hours would determine if he made it or not. He would have to be put in ICU to monitor further his condition where he spent the next sixteen days. When the hospital released him after a total of twenty-six days, they recommended a nursing home instead of releasing him to go to his house. The beating had left him unable to walk, and the nursing home would teach him to walk again.

My brother Larry and I found him a nursing home where Randy rehabilitated for twenty-eight days learning to walk again.

Daily visits every morning and evening gave Randy and me time to share some deep conversations. His life was getting ready to change for the better. God had the reins now.

Every day while visiting Randy in the nursing home, I would gently claim to him what Jesus had been doing in my life. Randy hadn't been to church in years. I wanted him to start coming with me every Sunday. I considered it my mission.

He realized the Lord had given him one more chance to live. Randy promised me he would start attending church with me again.

I was extremely excited about his choice. I purchased a new Bible for him to read while in the hospital. In the next few weeks, Randy was telling me how he was reciting verses from the Bible he never knew was in it. You could see Randy's love for the Lord was flowing from his very being. God was changing this man from the inside out.

We spoke of Randy's excessive use of alcohol up to this last event. I was so blessed to hear Randy tell me he didn't need to drink any longer, and the Lord was going to bring him away from his addiction, which He did.

The following March 2010, I asked Randy if he would like to have me sponsor him to attend a Walk To Emmaus weekend as I had done in May of 2009. He agreed to go, and his Emmaus experience set him on fire even more for the Lord. God's timing for Randy was perfect and right on time.

What a blessing it always is when Randy and I come across one of his old drinking buddies. They inform Randy how much better he looks and asks what has changed about him. He will immediately exclaim, "I have Jesus in my life now." He goes on to say how long he has now been without alcohol or drugs in his life.

God certainly worked a miracle in his life, and he lets everyone know about his love for Jesus. I am so blessed he is my brother.

Chapter 3

With six and one-half years separating us, Larry was the third-born son in our family. Working as a patrol officer for the Amarillo Police Department, Larry began his career when he turned twenty-one years old, and I was fifteen. I considered him my mentor during my teen years. I was the envy of all my friends because I had a brother who was a cop. I respected Larry and police officers, as did my friends. Having a cop brother made me more aware of the bad things criminals did. I wanted no part of it.

In those days, police officers held a higher level of respect. I wanted to be just like Larry. I guess you could say Larry was my Superman. Even better, my Superman was my real-life blood-brother.

In his uniform, he exuded authority. He wore a gun on his hip, but never placed his hand on it in a threatening manner.

Many times while in school, some of the kids talked about vandalizing the neighborhood. The very thing Larry was trying to protect citizens from, allowed me to see I never wanted to get into situations like the ones those kids wanted to do for "fun."

Larry and I were very close. He often included me in his activities as if there was no age gap between us. I was allowed to join him on a ride-along while he was on duty at the police department. Our relationship bonded and strengthened as we became closer.

One morning around midnight, while on a ride-along, we got into a high-speed chase involving a pickup truck. Exciting and scary at the same time was an understatement. We were patrolling a neighborhood where many new homes were under construction. Often the thieves broke in new dwellings, stealing ceiling fans, light fixtures, and removing the installed carpet from these homes.

The chase ensued for twenty minutes before the guys we were pursuing bailed out of the pickup in a rural area. There was no way of catching them as they ran on foot into the darkness. The criminals left the truck in drive, and it finally came to a stop when the pickup plowed into a tree.

While dogging these criminals at speeds up to one-hundred miles per hour, a person riding in the back of the pickup kept raising his head over the tailgate to see what was happening. I worried he might have a gun and start shooting at us. Thank goodness this didn't happen. However, in his haste to escape, he dropped his wallet in the bed of the truck, making it an easy crime to solve. Criminals are not always the smartest folks on the block.

The young man riding in the back of the pickup was only sixteen years old. Monday, he was arrested. During his interrogation, he gladly "ratted" out the others who were in the truck that early morning in exchange for leniency.

My brother received a certificate in his permanent file awarding him for solving this crime spree that had been perplexing the law authorities for several months.

Larry moved up in the ranks at the police department, becoming the rank of Sergent and taking many courses interesting to me. Larry became the first licensed arson investigator on the force. He shared some things he learned in arson school I would have never known if not for him.

Another certificate received by Larry was a certified handwriting analysis expert certificate. Larry was always an achiever, and it showed in his work with the police department.

I got to see firsthand how Larry handled even the worst criminals. He used respect for them as long as they were respectful to him. Watching him reminded me of how Jesus gave respect and love to people that were not so nice to Him. Larry loved people, and they knew it.

You could echo that Larry believed if you love God and love people, God will sort all the other things out later. I am so blessed Larry's love for the Lord made a massive influence on me and things you will read as you advance in this book.

Chapter 4

Throughout my school years, I never was concerned with being an honor student. I managed to squeak through high school with two goals on my mind; to graduate and learn more about automobiles. Two years of auto mechanics were the great classes I wanted from high school.

All my brothers had sharp muscle cars growing up. They would often take their hot rods to the local dragstrip to race down the quarter-mile track. Now, in high school, getting my driver's license was a goal I could achieve. Eagar on the tradition, I ran the dragstrip many times. My auto mechanics class gave me the ability to learn what made my car go faster. To this day, automobiles still intrigue me, and I love to tinker with them.

On the first day of high school, I found the chairs outside the vice-principals office and took a seat. Everyone knew these chairs were where a student would wait for discipline. Having three older brothers attend this school before me, I knew what I needed to do.

When the vice-principal approached the chairs, he took a seat beside me. Seeing his stature, you would have a mind of him being a former football coach because seated next to me; he loomed over me like a tall building and as full too. "Son, is there some way I could help you?" he asked.

I stood up, stuck my hand out to shake his and said, "Sir, I am Kim Barlow, the youngest of the Barlow boys, and

I don't want you to hold anything against me for what my brothers did at this school."

He chuckled as his giant hand swallowed mine in size. His smile showed his white, even teeth. "Son, you keep your nose clean, stay out of trouble, and you and I will get along just fine. You won't be back in these chairs."

Receiving swats was still allowed back then, and I didn't want to feel a single swat from this giant of a man. My brothers informed me he could swing a great paddle. I didn't need to think twice about behaving myself. Thankfully, I never had to visit him for discipline.

My first encounter with drugs was during my senior year. The auto mechanics shop was a large building with six-bay doors.

The auto shop teacher informed the class he had to retrieve supplies from the office. Our teacher had mentioned during class one day, he had lost his sense of smell—great news for one of my classmates, the pot-smoker.

Because the teacher couldn't smell, this allowed the classmate to smoke his pot in the farthest bay. Personally, it bothered me he would do this illegal act, but I didn't want to be a tattletale.

No sooner had the teacher left for the office, another classmate said, "Hey, Barlow, come over here. You can smoke some weed with us."

What would my parents and cop brother, Larry, think if I got caught? "No, thanks," I said, shaking my head and walking away.

During my junior year, I had met my high-school sweetheart Marcia. I often thought of my parents' many years of a happy marriage as something I also wanted. Marcia and I started to date, and I quickly had the sensation I was falling in love with her.

Hindsight tells me we were too young, and I think I was the one who brought up marriage. We both graduated in 1972, and by June of 1973, one year later, we were married.

My wife had juvenile diabetes. She had to take injections every day to control her blood sugar. This kind of diabetes can become a high-risk during pregnancy. The doctors told us she had one chance to give birth because her body could only stand this kind of trauma once. We discussed the danger and decided we did want a child.

Marcia became pregnant in March of 1975. When we looked for a Gyn/OB doctor, we found out there wasn't a qualified doctor in Amarillo who would take on this type of high-risk pregnancy. We were referred to a doctor in Lubbock who specialized in high-risk pregnancies. The 110-mile road between Amarillo and Lubbock became familiar to us traveling there many times for her appointments. Luckily Marcia had no complications during her term.

I am proud to proclaim the most beautiful blessing happened on January 6, 1976. Our beautiful, healthy daughter, Dawn, was born after a frantic drive to Lubbock. Dawn was our miracle and blessing from God.

Dawn has gone on to become an RN. She works as a pediatric ICU nurse in a local hospital. It melts my heart when someone discovers Dawn is my daughter. Everyone agrees she is the sweetest person they have ever met. I may be a little parti pris, but I must agree with them 100 percent.

I am saddened to say Dawn's mother, and I ended our marriage when our daughter was a young girl. I was such an immature young man back then. Had I been where I am now, especially in my walk with God, the divorce never would have happened. I wish I put more effort into what God had brought together than to throw this relationship away as I did.

I admire Marcia for raising such an outstanding woman as Dawn. I give God and her all the credit for the effort in building her to the high standards our daughter lives.

Forgiveness is the best form of love. My daughter, Dawn, would have every reason to hold onto the bitterness I created in her life. I was not present in her life growing up. But Dawn never gave up on me. She kept track of me through my brother Larry.

She would call my house before caller ID, only to hear my voice, and then disconnect the phone call.

Each day passing, we both were seeing the same catch-22 situation. I would think of calling Dawn, only to be side-tracked, thinking, *she won't want to talk to me*! If I call her, she will be so mad at me for missing out on her life; she will tell me never to call her again and hang up.

When I expressed this frustration to Dawn about those times wanting to call her, she represented the same frustrated feelings in those absent times from me. *He won't want to talk to me, and it will make him mad if I try,"* she said.

When Dawn and I speak of this time in our lives, my courageous daughter tells me, "I thank God you weren't around in that condition. Can you imagine how you would have acted when you were in your addiction around me?" Dawn has wisdom above her pay-grade.

I cannot show you how sacred it is to have Dawn's forgiveness, but also how she sees to it, we have a relationship now. I love my daughter with all my heart.

Our relationship proves to not focus on what's happened in our past. Focus on what God will do in our future. Having a bad start doesn't mean we can't have an exceptional finish. Our life today is more than what happened yesterday; it's about what we do with what happened yesterday. Whatever happened back then, we're now a new person.

Two years after Dawn's birth, I lost my father to cancer on April 22, 1978. I was twenty-four years old, and he was a young fifty-nine. His death made me feel short-changed because I would never have a dad to go to for advice and support. Going through a divorce was bad enough, but now I had truly lost my best friend too.

Our close relationship meant I could talk to him about anything. I realized Dad's age gave him much wisdom to teach if only I would listen. Many nights I cried myself to sleep grieving over my father's death.

Dad's close friend, Roy Wheeler, a pastor, saw me at the grocery store a few months following Daddy's passing. We hugged and started chatting. Roy asked how I was getting along. A tear rolled down my cheek as I described how I was still hurting, trying to heal from Daddy's death. He handed me a tissue to dry my tears. Roy put his hand on my shoulder and told me something which has stuck with me all my life.

Roy said, "Kim, I know it is hard losing your dad, but God needed him worse than we did." Those words were the first thing that made sense to me why the Lord took my dad at such a young age. As time passed, the hurt became more comfortable, but it remains.

My dad left behind a beautiful legacy. I firmly believe my Dad is in heaven and because he enjoyed life so much, I know he is going to delight in paradise even more. He will breathe the pure sweet air, and savor every beautiful thing there because he conditioned himself here to adore the beautifulness of earth. Daddy loved people, and they felt it. Jesus found it precious in His eyes to see one of His children returning home.

After this many years have gone by since Daddy's death, people continue to remark, "I loved your Dad. He was a great guy."

To see Jesus will be heavens' greatest joy. What a glorious reunion it will be one day soon. Save me a seat up there, Daddy. I will see you soon.

With Joe on the way to my house, yelling out he was going to kill me, it could be sooner than I anticipated.

Chapter 5

I have always held a job, tried to do what was right, and managed to get along with everyone. If I had to name my biggest fault, it would be trying to be a "people-pleaser."

In 1989, I met a woman. We will call her Nancy. We married in June of 1990. I had a great job with a major company and was making good money. My wife brought her two children from another marriage into this relationship, and we were one big, happy family.

Nancy had always struggled to make ends meet. Being a single parent providing for her two children was not easy. All of them wore clothes which looked second-hand to me. Our first Christmas together before we were married, I bought each member of my new family a brand-new wardrobe. It made my heart full of joy to provide for her and the kids. I could tell this woman needed me, and I needed someone to care for in my life.

Three months into our marriage, Nancy and I decided to host a Saturday get-together at our home. We had invited my wife's two older sisters to join us along with their husbands. Nancy's family had accepted me as one of their own. Spending time at each other's homes on the weekends grew to be commonplace.

A typical Saturday evening party, Nancy and I offered alcohol, snacks, and food. While the family assembled in the kitchen, my two brothers-in-law, Dave and Richard, made their way through the side door into the garage. By this time, all our inhibitions had numbed by the alcohol, and the whiskey and colas I had consumed all evening. Past midnight, I wondered about Dave and Richard's absence into the garage, but I wasn't that concerned.

A few minutes later, the door opened. Dave stuck his head inside and said, "Hey, Barlow, come out here a minute. We want to show you something."

I was suspicious as to why they wanted to show me something in my garage? Wanting to keep everyone happy, I pushed my doubt aside and followed him into the garage.

Once in the garage, I asked my brothers-in-law, "What are you guys doing out here?" They motioned me to the hood of my car, where I quickly noticed two lines of a whitish-amber powder drawn out on the shiny hood of my car.

"Barlow, try some of this. Take this straw and sniff it into your nose," Dave insisted.

These two burly truck drivers were trying to lure me into something I had never done before. I distinctively didn't want to take part in this.

My mind began racing, thinking, *What would Larry feel about me doing this?* I knew this was something illegal, but I also wanted to fit in.

These guy's professions were what they call "bull-haulers," driving cattle trucks across the country. Back then, truckers were notorious for doing drugs to keep them awake to encourage working abnormally long hours. I was apprehensive. My human mind cautioned not to make my new family members find reasons not to like me.

"I have never done anything like this." I sternly added, "There's no way I'm going to do that now or ever." I didn't even know what this powder spread out on the hood of my car was, but my gut feeling said it wasn't something good.

I didn't want to partake in consuming drugs. My brother, Larry's face, kept flashing through my mind. Larry would not approve of this taking place. I could sense what his disappointment would have been had he known.

My two brothers-in-law were shaking their heads like they couldn't believe I wasn't anxious to join in. They were offering me an escape. I soon learned these guys were not going to take no for an answer. The more I resisted, the more the peer pressure thickened.

"You're a chicken! You're a grown man! It's just speed. Don't be a girl! Come on, man, it isn't going to hurt you," they hissed.

"Kim, we do this all the time. Don't worry about it," David said. "Hell, it may not do a thing to you."

All lies while trying to lure me into their misery.

These two were offering me seemingly powerless pressure, making me feel less. I wanted to belong. I needed to belong. The feeling was I did not fit in the family if I didn't go along with them.

The aggravation from my two brothers-in-law, and the alcohol combined had me believing those two lines of powder weren't going to hurt me if I snorted them just once.

Maybe it won't hurt me, I was saying in my mind. Do it, and the brothers-in-law will stop insisting.

Knowing nothing about such things, I asked Dave to go first so I could watch. He put the straw about an eighth of an inch into one of his nostrils. He leaned over to put the straw into the powder on the hood. He started to inhale the dust up the straw and into his nose. He steadily moved the straw along the length of the line before handing the straw to me. The range of powder is typically about three inches long.

I was certainly curious if it were true what Dave and Richard had said. Was this going to kill me? Or was this simply a recreational thing done for fun? After all, Dave had done it in front of me. He didn't turn into a monster. Maybe it was more like taking a shot of whiskey. I decided it was time.

I leaned down, I placed the straw up my nose, then started to snort it briskly as I moved it along the three-inch line. As I sucked it into my nose, the powder burned the inside of my nostrils as if I had jalapeno powder up my nose. Tears began to stream down my cheeks. The burning sensation lasted about forty-five seconds. Why would anyone torture themselves this way?

The next thing to come was the nasty taste drenching down the back of my throat. The most bitter and most disgusting taste made me gag. I wondered, *Who could enjoy this?* It was then, and I insisted they tell me what I had put up my nose.

The powder I had snorted had many street names, crank, ice, speed, or crystal. The generic of these is called methamphetamine, often referred to as, "The devil's drug."

There are many different procedures to ingest meth. The people who manufacture meth, make it into a block, which is then broken off into what is called "rock." This rock can, when crushed, be made into a powder to snort up the nose, or it can be mixed with water to and injected into a vein. Some take a piece of rock and wrap it in tissue, then swallow it like a pill. My choice during my addiction was to smoke my meth in a glass pipe made from a Pyrex glass test tube.

I frequented a hobby house in my town where people who smoked their meth would purchase five-inch Pyrex test tubes. I often wondered if employees of the hobby store knew why they sold so many five-inch test tubes?

I took pleasure in making a pipe from the glass. It involved using a hand-held torch using a gas called Mapp gas. This bottle torch would heat the tube to the melting point. Turning red indicated it was melting to a point you could blow easily into the open end.

Blowing into the open end would start the tube to form a bulb as the glass expanded. When the desired bulb formed, blowing hard on the molten end would blow out a small vent hole in the bulb end of the pipe. This vent was necessary when smoking meth from the tube.

Dropping a small rock into the bulb end was the first step to smoke it. Using a lighter or butane torch beneath the bulb caused the meth to start to boil and burn. At this point, you would inhale the smoke-producing in the pipe.

Everyone had to learn to be cautious when heating meth to smoke as it is extremely flammable. While heating the meth in the pipe, if it's too hot, it will flash into a fireball, and fire will be in your lungs before you can stop it. There were so many things wrong about doing meth, but it had me hooked from the first time.

I had many chances to shoot meth into my veins. I watched as many did it in front of me. Every single one that took meth in their veins always invited me to try it too. They said the high was much more significant if I were to shoot it up in my veins.

Previous medical training as an EMT made me hesitate to use needles. I knew I didn't want to inject anything into my veins, which weren't often sterile. While observing others shooting up, I realized there wasn't anything pure about this act.

The "shooters" would crush the meth in a spoon and add tap water to dissolve the rock. Using a cigarette filter to filter the liquid into a syringe, stick it in a vein, and release the meth was the standard practice. To me, this seemed suicidal.

I thank God He gave me the wisdom to never shoot up meth. Though smoking, it wasn't healthier, it offered me a better chance at survival.

There are strong arguments why meth is called "The devil's drug." For most, it hooks the user from the very first use, and the addiction can be impossible to overcome.

I have observed different users who use meth intravenously, are the ones who have the hardest time getting rid of their addiction. Because intravenous users receive such large doses, they are frequently the ones you hear in the news doing horrible things to secure their drug money and while under the influence.

I had a choice this night in the garage and could hold no one accountable for my actions except me. What I didn't realize, was how powerful the "Devils drug" would become to me.

Chapter 6

Only three days had passed since smoking my first meth. By Wednesday of the next week, I was feeling the need for more. My body and mind craved the feeling like the very first time. The euphoria of not requiring sleep and an energy level that won't stop was invigorating. The down-side was the difficulty of concentrating on one task at a time.

Any meth addict will tell you; they are always trying to "chase" the first time high. The rush of energy traveling through the body like an electric shock is motivating.

Cleaning your house from top to bottom is common. Maybe you'll do it twice! The problem with all this energy? Unable to concentrate on one thing at a time, the mind races ahead to the next task. You may never finish one job before starting another. I know it sounds idiotic, but this was the feeling my mind and body wanted again.

By the next Saturday, we decided to have another get-together. I was hoping for more meth to feel this energy level again. My brother-in-law brought more meth. We went into the garage and repeated the scenario all over again.

In the beginning, I started using only on weekends. After a couple of days, my mind was telling me, no matter how badly I didn't want to do it, I needed more meth to function. Without the meth, all I wanted to do is sleep. My energy level disappeared when I hadn't smoked meth in a few hours.

Meth corrals users into a no-win situation. The need to miss sleep for two or three days is real. If trying to stop using meth for even a day, all your body wants to do is catch up on the sleep you lost. I'd become so sluggish from the lack of sleep I couldn't function. Once laying down to finally sleep, except for having to wake up to go to the bathroom, I often slept for twelve or more hours at a time.

About a month had passed before I was asking my brothers-in-law where *I* could buy some meth for myself instead of bothering them. They talked it over and decided to introduce me to *the* dealer who supplied their drugs.

It was a secret brotherhood being able to meet a dealer.

It required them to tell the dealer a little about me and to make him know I was safe to bring me around him. I called it back then, "The good ole-boys network."

I had the appearance of a "clean-cut" guy. Paranoid drug dealers don't like clean-cut guys. Dealers see clean-cut guys as undercover cops. Being new to the addiction, I didn't look like a typical meth-head. I didn't appear spaced-out and tweaking. If my brothers-in-law hadn't personally taken me there, I would have never made it through the dealer's door. At the time, I was appreciative.

Getting "hooked up" with a dealer enabled me to buy larger quantities of meth, and larger quantities available made it easier to do it more often. I soon noticed my body craved more and more. My weekend use turned into an every-other-day need, and then within a few weeks, a daily requirement. If I didn't have meth, my energy level evaporated. All I wanted to do was sleep. Smoking every day became part of my life.

During my addiction, I admitted I'd become a "functional addict." I had a job and other responsibilities I had to take care of while on dope. Because I had those responsibilities, it did not mean I took care of those responsibilities well. My wife and I found our addiction turning into a one-hundred-dollar a week habit.

Two of Nancy's sisters used meth also. I know that Nancy most likely had participated in using before she met me. The two sisters I am speaking of was married to David and Richard, Nancy's brothers-in-law. This time in my life was going to be the beginning of a potent addiction and a different course for my livelihood. Meth had me hooked, and I couldn't stop now.

Chapter 7

It was 1994, and Nancy and I had finished building our second custom home. I was showing my wife a life she had never experienced, and her family had introduced me to a life I had never experienced.

Nancy and I became close friends with Billy and his wife Sherry (not their real names). Billy was the manager of the company store where he and I worked. I was the outside salesman, while Billy took care of store operations.

One day I mentioned, "Billy, we should all get together for a party." We started discussing what we would cook, what alcohol we preferred, and what entertainment we would have.

During our conversation, as men will talk about, we chatted about parties in our past and how drunk we became. In our one-up-manship, I happened to mention how much I enjoyed meth in the past. Billy had no idea I was using meth at the time we were talking. He said it had been a while since he had consumed any drugs, but he sure enjoyed meth in the past also.

Of course, misery loves company, so I mentioned Nancy, and I had some meth stashed at the house.

With the Labor Day weekend approaching, I invited Billy and Sherry over for a get-together during the entire weekend and to party if we wanted. They were excited about the idea of partying with Nancy and I. Because of the holiday, and our store closed on Saturday, Sunday, and Monday, allowing us to party all these days if we wished.

Billy and Sherry came to our home on Friday evening. We started the evening cooking out, and soon after eating, we started playing card games and consuming alcohol. If you were on meth, you never felt drunk. Alcohol is a depressant, and meth is a stimulant, so they counteract each other.

About midnight, I told Billy I wanted to show him something in my bedroom. We excused ourselves and left the girls talking in the kitchen.

I brought Billy into the large master bathroom where I had some meth in my pipe ready to smoke. We smoked some and went back to where the girls were. On the way back to the kitchen, Billy asked if he could bring his wife back there to smoke some too. "Of course," I answered.

The thing about using meth means staying awake sometimes for two or more days at a time. All four of us had smoked meth, and the next thing we knew, the sun was rising in the eastern sky. We were still partying. We could not believe we weren't tired at all. By 7:30 AM, our guests decided to go home. We had such a great time, my wife and I invited them back this same evening.

It was Saturday morning, and I needed to contact my meth dealer because we had used my supply of meth the night before. Our friends wondered if I would get them an amount too, and they would pay me when they came back to our house this evening.

Saturday evening, when they arrived, they told us they had stayed up all day and didn't feel tired at all. We were not surprised by their feelings.

After cooking out, the card games began, along with alcohol consumption. About 9:00 PM, I brought the meth out. We smoked it at the table while playing card games, drinking alcohol while having a great evening with our friends.

It was 3:00 AM when Billy and Sherry strangely announced they wanted to journey off to our master bathroom together. It was a large area we had custom-built to the size of a small bedroom.

Thirty minutes had passed, when my wife and I wondered why they had been in the master bathroom this long? I went to the bathroom door to ask if they were okay? Billy said they were okay and would be out in a few minutes.

After another half-hour passed, I went back to the bathroom. Standing in front of the door, I loudly said, "Let me in, or I'm going to break the door down." I waited a few seconds until Billy came to the door and opened it.

When Billy opened the door, he and Sherry looked like lepers! I asked them what the hell were they doing? During the time they were in the bathroom, they picked many spots on their faces and arms until they bled. I am not speaking of two or three places. They were like every three inches on all exposed bare skin. Billy started to convince me worms were crawling out from their skin, and they were pulling them out of their skin with their fingernails, causing bloody sores everywhere they had picked their skin.

The next time you watch a reality cop show, this is a sign some meth users encounter. When people arrested for possession of meth, observe their faces and arms. Many times, you will see "sores" where they "picked" at their bodies. I have so many reasons to thank God He protected Nancy and me with His grace and mercy, thankful I never reacted such as this.

Billy and Sherry swore they were picking worms out of their skin. He had me look at a few of those spots, to see if I could also see the worms sticking out from the surface. These two looked like a living monster. These signs were an indication of too much meth ingested and too much sleep deprivation. Usually, Billy and Sherry were an attractive couple. Billy and Sherry's sores were going to be evident to everyone; *something wasn't right with them.*

Sunday morning around 7:00 AM, I announced, "The party's over, and I'm taking you two home to go to bed." I loaded them up in my vehicle to take them home.

Billy had to be back to work on Tuesday. He called in sick Tuesday but showed up to work on Wednesday. His story to everyone as he had a bad rash break out. Somehow no one questioned poor Billy, but we never had them over to our home again.

Sometimes tricky situations make me feel like I want to run away. That desperation to find relief temps me to take things in my own hands. I could fix all my problems myself—just a matter of willpower.

Thank God, He redeems our failures and uses them for His glory. The things you remember with shame now become examples of God's amazing grace and power to transform lives.

Chapter 8

In 1995, the company I worked for asked if I would be interested in taking over the entire state of New Mexico as the outside sales rep. The town we would move to was Albuquerque.

The company offered me an excellent transfer package, including buying our new home and taking care of all our moving expenses. I was apprehensive at first, never living anywhere except my hometown. My wife and I discussed the prospect, and we're excited about moving to a new area.

The company flew me to Denver to interview with my new boss. After speaking with him, I quickly knew this was going to be a great break I couldn't refuse.

My wife and I had visited Albuquerque before and enjoyed the culture there. Albuquerque has excellent Mexican food restaurants, and the American Indian culture had always intrigued me. The land was beautiful due to the mountain range on the Eastern edge of Albuquerque.

The mountain range is named "Sandia," which translates to "watermelon." As the sun would set in the western skies, a watermelon color draped over the mountain range to the east, creating a beautiful sight.

On top of Sandia Peak was an excellent ski area for winter fun. All season long, you can take a tramway to the top, providing a magnificent view of Albuquerque below. The Sandia Peak Tramway is the longest spanning tramway in

America. Sandia Peak Tram takes visitors 2.7 miles or 10,378 feet up the Sandia Mountains.

One of our significant concerns was our addiction. We panicked, wondering where we would get our meth? Two hundred and sixty-five miles from Amarillo and from our supplier, a four-hour drive to Amarillo and then a four-hour return drive wasn't plausible.

After I accepted the job, another major problem arose.

Accepting the new position required me to change regions. While in Amarillo, I was in the Southern region. Now I was part of the Southwest region.

My new boss said changing regions meant the company considered me a "new-hire." I would need to take a "mini" physical, including a drug test. My heart sunk when I heard the words *drug test*.

My mind raced. How could I pass a drug test after being on meth for five years? I didn't know if I could quit, much less if the drug use would show up in the results?

All I could think of was what would happen if I tested positive for meth? I couldn't help imagining how disappointed my cop-brother, Larry, would be finding out. I was about to have my life ruined, and my career forever.

In a panic, Nancy and I started to ask people we did dope with what to do? Everyone assured us, if I quit meth for two weeks, and drink lots of water, all the narcotics would flush out of my system. My online research agreed. I knew I had to do this because my drug test was three weeks out.

The next three weeks were a living hell. Withdrawing was a challenging thing. All I wanted to do was sleep, and I had zero energy. This symptom was very typical to those removing from meth use. My meth intake at the time was luckily not near the input I would experience in the years to come.

During those three weeks, my routine consisted of coming home from work, eat dinner, and go to bed until the next morning. I was very tempted to take one more smoke of meth but knew I couldn't. My only choice? Get through this or be fired.

Three long weeks passed, and it was time to take my physical. I hoped my research was correct, or I was going to be doomed. I can't describe what anxiety looks like, but I knew I experienced it at the doctor's office. I gave my urine specimen to the nurse and said a prayer, "Lord, please let me pass this test."

My boss called me the next day to congratulate me. I had passed the physical. This news felt like a ton had lifted off my shoulders. I thanked the Lord for getting me through this time.

My company gave us six weeks before the moving van came to transfer our belongings for the trip to Albuquerque. The six weeks ahead of our relocation, my company put me in a beautiful corporate apartment while I searched for a home for us. Nancy stayed in Amarillo packing and getting our belongings ready for the transfer.

I found a place in Rio Rancho, a suburb on the Northwest side of Albuquerque. Nancy and I had such a great connection, and she knew whatever home I picked out, she would be okay with it. Our house faced east looking at the Sandia mountains. We would witness a beautiful watermelon-colored sunset almost every evening. Our home felt terrific, and we felt like we had made the right decision to move.

Only one thing left. We needed a local dealer in the area to purchase our meth. We seemed to make this priority number one. It wasn't like you could walk up to anyone and ask, "Do you know where we could buy some meth?" The supply we had brought from our previous home was running out fast. What were we going to do?

Chapter 9

Things began falling in place at my new job. The first week consisted of meeting my new customers and getting acquainted with my new co-workers. I liked my new co-workers in Albuquerque. Taking this promotion was the right decision.

The first days of a job seem somewhat uncomfortable finding the rhythm of how things operate. On Thursday of the first week, one of my co-workers came to me to say, "Kim, on Friday evenings, we buy some beer and drink a couple after closing time." Being invited to join them and gave me the feeling of fitting in as "one of the guys." I was looking forward to Friday evening.

Friday at 6:00 PM, we locked the front doors. In the back warehouse, hidden from visibility, was a table with chairs where we could sit. Someone had purchased a small refrigerator to store food for lunches, but its primary use was for Friday evening's "beer-time."

We each grabbed a beer and gathered around the table. We had a great time chatting and talking about how well the week had gone. Conversation flowed easily.

As men will sometimes do, it was a typical "guy" talk conversation. After a couple of beers, we began sharing some of the stupid things we did while drinking alcohol. We soon were trying to "one-up" each other's story, as men often will do.

Toward the end of our evening, I was feeling a small buzz. I told my co-workers although my drunken times were fun, I mentioned I had done some drugs in my past, and I loved the high I had from meth.

Immediately, one of my co-workers, Bobby, said, "Kim, are you telling me you have done meth before?" I explained how deep I was into meth back in Amarillo. Curiously, I asked Bobby, "Why do you ask if I have done meth before?" It was then he said in a hushed voice, "Well, my brother-in-law is a 'cook,' and anytime I wanted some to let him know."

A "cook" is someone who manufactures meth in a lab like in a spare bedroom or their garage. It is very dangerous to make meth because the mixture, if not done, correctly becomes a stick of dynamite. There have been many "cooks" who blow themselves up manufacturing meth. Two of the volatile chemicals used making meth is a thinner called, Acetone, and the other one is Ether. Both of these chemicals are so flammable, static electricity from touching another object close by can start a volatile fire.

I had always known in the drug world, the closer you are to the manufacturer, the stronger the drug. Some dealers take the pure meth, and "cut" it many times before it gets to the end-user.

Greedy dealers will take the potent meth, and mix it with things like baby laxatives, or even Sweet-and-low to make him more money from his stash.

When Bobby said I could get some meth from a cook, I thought I had died and gone to heaven, and it would be the first time I'd be able to get my meth straight from the maker.

Before we left the store, I walked over to Bobby as he was getting in his car and asked him, "How long would it take you to get me some of this good meth you were speaking of?" He said he would bring it to work the next morning.

I had been clean from meth starting on my fourth week, but I was craving the "first-high" experience again. At home, I told Nancy the excellent news. She showed joy in knowing we had found a source for our addiction. We were getting ready to cave-in to feed our addictions as it had never been before.

The next morning, Bobby brought a gram of meth as promised. Finally, our predicament in Albuquerque was over. I could hardly wait to get home to smoke some with Nancy.

Once home, I found my glass pipe, dropped a little rock in it, and started smoking. Our meth was stronger than it had ever been before. I sympathize with alcoholics at meetings; they are told, "Don't ever take one drink, or you will be right where you left off when you were an alcoholic." The same thing applied to our meth use. We, too, were right back where we had left off!

Chapter 10

By 1998, my wife and I had been in Albuquerque for about two and one-half years, and a series of things started to happen. The company I worked for sold to a company out of England. The new company was making it impossible for me to do business as usual. All employees received a letter stating every employee's salaries were frozen for one year to return more money to the shareholders in England. Nancy and I knew we needed more money for our new addiction, causing me to start searching for another job.

I communicated with Nancy how unhappy I was with my job since the company takeover. We knew we could find a way to make it back in Amarillo if we had to. She was very supportive of me and trusted me to make the right decision.

A couple of weeks before I quit my job in 1998, I decided to reach out to my oldest brother, Scotty, in Amarillo. He mentioned he had a man approach him to acquire a small "tote the note" car lot in Amarillo. Tote-the-note meaning he would finance the cars sold to a customer. He wanted to bring me in as a partner.

Scotty was my firstborn brother leaving ten-years between our ages. He had been a car salesman all his life. His experience included the General Manager of several large dealerships in Amarillo, Lubbock, and Dallas. I always looked up to Scotty as being one of the best salesmen I knew.

Losing my Dad when I was twenty-four years old, I now looked to Scotty as my father-figure.

Unfortunately, Scotty had not been the most trust-worthy person in his life. A few weeks before the call, Scotty recently was released from federal prison.

He had been serving an eighteen-month sentence for bank fraud. He and another man were charged and convicted with swindling a Federal Credit Union out of three-hundred and eighty-five thousand dollars.

After hanging up with Scotty, I called my other two brothers back in Amarillo. Separately, I asked each of them if they thought Scotty had learned his lesson while in prison? Each echoed Scotty had changed. I, too, had the feeling he was on the up-and-up about the car lot he wanted me to invest in with him.

I discussed with Nancy about quitting my job and moving back to Amarillo to pursue this new chapter of being a used car dealer. The plan included Nancy staying behind in Rio Rancho and sell the house. After it sold, I would come and move us all back to Amarillo. We both agreed this was the best plan of action.

The money I'd saved up in a retirement account, I withdrew. I had saved $32,000 to put in this car lot. I soon found out the IRS takes 33 percent right off the top as a penalty for taking your retirement early. Still, I was determined to make this work for my family.

I packed and took off for Amarillo. My mother offered me to move in with her temporarily until the car-lot became profitable. She lived alone and was happy to have her "baby boy" living with her.

I had been partners at the car lot for about six months when I had to admit it was not taking off like my brother promised it would. I was quickly going broke. Nancy was having no luck selling the home in Rio Rancho. Our bills kept coming, and we were struggling paying them without my income.

I was running out of money, and I expressed this to Scotty. His answer was for me to get cash advances on all my credit cards because the car lot was going to hit the jackpot any day.

I wanted to give my brother the benefit-of-the-doubt, but instead, he was lining his own pockets, while I ran up a considerable debt to the tune of eighty-five-thousand-dollars.

While in Amarillo, trying to make money at this car lot, Nancy worked at an insurance agency and was attempting to make ends meet there. Unfortunately, without my income and us building up such a massive debt, things spiraled downward fast.

Creditors constantly bombarded us with calls and letters stating they were going to start foreclosure proceedings on our home in Rio Rancho. Collectors are relentless and could care less about the excuses as to why you can't pay your debt.

The time came had come. Our mortgage lender warned us they were starting foreclosure proceedings on our home in Rio Rancho.

With no choice left, I rented a moving truck and loaded up everything to bring it back to Amarillo. The bank foreclosed on the house in Rio Rancho. They continued harassment relentlessly, wanting their $185,000 back from the foreclosure.

Nancy and I were struggling in our marriage, too. I wasn't making much money with my brother at the car lot, and to make matters worse, the bank repossessed my wife's automobile. We eventually divorced and went our separate ways. I felt a real low in my life. I was a complete failure.

Depression, led by stress, was now a part of my life. Creditors kept up their nasty, threatening calls. I had so little money I can recall wanting a can of soda so much, and I could taste it. But I didn't have a cent to my name until payday on Friday. A canned drink was fifty cents, and I couldn't scrape enough together to buy one.

I had to admit the car lot was going to land me on the streets homeless if I didn't leave this job—a hard lesson to learn. My confidence was in the gutter.

I found employment with a mobile home company as a salesman. I worked seventy hours a week and making less than minimum wages—the lifestyle I had grown used to while in Albuquerque, was now shattered, in a rut, and getting deeper. *How was I ever going to get out of it?*

In 2002, I recalled my roots as a flooring salesman. I had nothing to lose by asking a former flooring company if they would rehire me.

I made an appointment with the owner, and he hired me on the spot. I was blessed things might be looking up for a change.

I was happy at the flooring company. I was not only making money again, but it gave me the chance to buy and consume more meth.

While working at the flooring company, the owner of another flooring company contacted me several times, wanting me to come work for him. Feeling secure at the company I worked for, I shrugged off his offers.

By October of 2005, my boss hired a consultation company to increase the company's efficiency. The most significant expense a company has is its employees. The consultation company convinced the owner to cut every salesman's commission by 6 percent.

At this time, I was the companies highest-volume sales-man. My record revealed I was a great salesman, even while high on meth.

My employer often invited me for a chat in his office. He would mention more than once, "Kim, I don't need any-one to take drug testing around here. I can spot them a mile away." *Really? I was high on meth every day I worked at his store.*

After the consultation company gave the owner the plan of action, he scheduled a meeting with all the salesmen. He explained he would cut our commissions by 6 percent.

The next day I asked him for a private meeting with me. I explained I couldn't make it on a 6 percent cut in my commission. He told me, "Kim, stick around for a month or two. You will see you won't even notice the difference in pay." I may have been high on meth, but I knew this was wrong.

I stayed at this flooring company until December notic-ing a sizable drop in my pay. I started talking seriously with the owner of the competing flooring company. After our ini-tial meeting, he made me a reasonable offer. I resigned from my job the week after Christmas and started with the new company in January of 2005.

From 2005 until 2008 was a time I was at my peak drug use. At my new job, I continually made mistakes. I would order the wrong color carpet, or maybe request a different flooring than the customer had chosen. The meth was taking over my sound judgment, and frustration was the new nor-mal. The meth use was starting to take a toll. The owner of the flooring company was undoubtedly disappointed, but no more than me.

Up for three or more days without sleep, unintended, I would doze off at my computer desk at home. One early morning I looked at the clock noting it was 2:00 AM. Next,

I was awakening to the sun shining through my windows, wondering if I'd fallen asleep? I glanced at the clock to discover it read nine thirty.

My mind was so foggy, I panicked. My heart raced as I wondered if it were 9:30 AM or PM? I flipped through TV channels and realized morning news programs filled the central station. My workplace opened at 8:00 AM, and I was an hour and a half late!

My boss was a punctual person. Being late many times and making mistakes ordering the wrong flooring, why hadn't he fired me? Spiraling out of control, errors on my part had become the new normal.

As I entered work over two hours late, I hoped I could sneak past the people in charge. Of course, this was false thinking. My boss invited me to his office, where I apologized, explaining to him I had a sleep disorder. Thankfully, one more lie to him soothed him with my answer.

The owner's sister, Ruth, was our store manager. Our front counter was about four feet tall, so it was a comfortable place to put your arms on while you were chatting with someone or for relaxing.

Ruth stood on one end of the counter while I was on the opposite end. We were making small talk, when suddenly she yelled out, "Kim Barlow, did you just fall asleep on me?" I jerked upright.

I had fallen asleep standing up while listening to her. I was so embarrassed. I apologized, using the same lie I was experiencing some sleep disorders.

In the drug culture, this disorder is called "zoning out." To explain zoning out, have you relaxed in front of the TV, your eyelids become heavy, and you suddenly nod off? You perhaps may start snoring?

Zoning out is different from your eyelids getting heavy. Zoning out happens due to a lack of sleep. The brain instructs the body, "Body, you are going to go to sleep right now!" No notice, no heavy eyelids, your eyes shut, and your head drops to your chest! You have lost all control. I had zoned out, standing upright while chatting with Ruth.

Sleep deprivation does harsh things to your body. There is *nothing* you can do to control it but get some sleep. The trap is, you don't want to go to sleep while you are high on meth.

After several days awake, I remember while walking through the kitchen at my home, and I felt my knees buckle. I had fallen asleep while walking. Thank God, for some reason, my eyes opened, and I caught myself before I fell to the ground.

Once at work, I sat down with a female customer at a table in the store. I started to show her some samples, and the next thing I knew, someone tugged on my sleeve.

I awoke to a voice, asking, "Sir, sir, are you okay? You were talking to me, and your head fell to your chest like you had fallen asleep!"

I apologized, expressing how sorry I was, and explained I had been experiencing some sleep problems. I knew my addiction was in control of me, but not enough to give up my addiction to meth.

Selling meth was paying for my addiction, but more cash meant I increased my use even more. I didn't like the business of selling meth. I knew I was one minute away from getting busted every time I made a sale.

Around this time, I recognized the true colors of some addictions. I hate to admit this, but I was selling to people who were so desolate, they were stealing to get their next fix.

An example of how there is no honor among thieves? One evening, a couple who were dating came to my home to purchase meth. I sold to the female several times before, but this was the first time I met her boyfriend. Usually, we would sit at my dining room table. Commonly the dealer let the customer have a small sample of the meth.

After we smoked a sample, I excused myself to go to the bathroom. I couldn't have gone for more than two minutes. I trusted the female because she had been a customer of mine for a few months. When I got back to the table, they acted like they were suddenly in a hurry to get out of my house, saying, "We better get going. Thanks for the dope, Kim."

The next evening, I grimaced, glancing at my entertainment center. I owned a very nice Panasonic hand-held video camera I stored next to the TV. Now the camera was nowhere in sight. I searched everywhere for the video camera.

Where had I put the camera? It was right here the last time I saw it. And then, the reality sank in. My "friends" stole from me. Tears filled my eyes.

In a cabinet, I discovered they had also taken my "still-picture" camera, too. This camera was a Canon AE1 with a big telephoto lens attachment in a carrying case, and I was so proud to have this camera. I called the couple many times, but they never answered or returned my calls. Both cameras were gone, and I would never see them again, proving there is no honor among thieves.

Chapter 11

The following is an example I'm not proud to share, but it exemplifies the ways of a meth addict.

On my day off during the week, I knew my sweet mother would be awake early in the morning. About 6:30 AM, I called her to see if I could come by for a visit. It had been a couple of weeks since our last visit. She offered to cook me some breakfast.

Arriving fifteen minutes later, Mother invited me in and motioned for me to have a seat on the couch while she fixed bacon, hash-browns, toast, and eggs. She handed me a cup of coffee and said breakfast would be ready soon.

I relaxed on her couch, while the scent of bacon rolled through the house. Mother was an excellent cook, and every-thing always tasted better when she prepared it. I was sure this would be no exception.

Instead of eating at her dining room table, she brought me a big overstuffed pillow to put on my lap to act as a TV tray.

Her thoughtfulness allowed me to eat my breakfast right there on the couch. Soon, my mother served my break-fast plate, sitting it on the pillow in my lap.

Mother knew nothing about my addiction, nor did she know her baby boy had been up several days before coming to visit her.

I took a couple of bites, and the next thing I knew, my mother was saying, "Kim! Kim!" She had both hands on the side of my head as she lifted my head from the plate.

I had zoned out, and I landed face-first into the eggs. When I raised my head, busted egg yolks had spread across my face. Mother brought a clean towel and dabbed at my face. She asked me if I had been working too hard or not getting enough sleep? I told her that was the reason and left it at that. But the truth was, I was doing way too much meth and *not* getting enough sleep.

Sometimes after staying awake for two or three days, I had to smoke more and more meth to function. I could feel my heart racing and pound in my chest. At times my heart pounded so hard, I thought any minute, "Kim, you are getting ready to die."

Feeling the strength of the addiction, getting ready to die didn't stop me. Although I said to my drug buddies, "You know I could quit this anytime I want to, but I just like it too much."

Satan was whispering the worn-out tactics he uses in every battle. He deceives, lies, accuses, and seeks to destroy us all.

The truth was, if my drug buddies really cared about my well-being and were my real friends, they would have been trying as hard as they could to get me off drugs, instead of worrying where their next fix was. Unfortunately, they were in the same deadlock as me.

Many times I perceived myself as an insignificant speck lost in this enormous world. But Jesus knows us by name. He knows our past; He knows what we will face in the future, and because He knows everything about us, His word to us will perfectly fit the circumstances of our life.

God will personalize His word to us. He will relate to each of our friends in a way that specifically meets their needs as well. I felt terrible about the lies I had to act out with everyone, including my mother. But still not awful enough to stop the insanity of my addiction.

Chapter 12

Almost every meth addict develops what is called "meth-mouth." I'm not a doctor, but I believe meth-mouth involves practicing some of the following techniques:

The teeth of people addicted to methamphetamines are noticeable by teeth blackening, stained, rotting, crumbling, and falling apart. The teeth become so deteriorated the teeth must be pulled. The extensive tooth decay is also likely caused by a combination of drug-induced psychological and physiological changes resulting in dry mouth. Methamphetamine itself is too acidic.

The more meth a person uses, the worse their teeth decay. Meth users who are thirty years of age or older, women and cigarette smokers were more likely to have tooth decay and gum disease. I smoked cigarettes during this time, thus adding to the problem.

The high (which causes the brain to feel intense pleasure) can last up to twelve hours. While high, users often crave high-calorie, carbonated, sugary beverages. Also, they may grind or clench their teeth, all of which can harm teeth. Meth users regularly practice poor dental hygiene.

Meth-mouth causes every tooth in your head to become loose. They fall out of the gums one by one. The pain sometimes was so excruciating I would cry as one by one, my teeth would rock back and forth as they become loose in my gums. Even drinking tap water was too sensitive to drink because it felt too cold on my teeth. My addiction was hurting my body physically, and I knew it but couldn't seem to break the habit.

Often, I would be eating a meal and bite down on something hard like a piece of gravel. I would reach into my mouth to discover another tooth had fallen out of my gums. Eventually, this led to having my remaining teeth pulled, and full dentures now fill my mouth.

This small thorn in my mouth holds no to comparison to the grace and mercy Jesus showed taking me out of my addiction.

I was the obstacle standing in God's way.

Chapter 13

By May of 2008, meth had me locked in my addiction for eighteen years. My life was spiraling out of control. Paranoia erupted, clouding any happiness. I always worried I could have the police bust through my door at any minute. I was selling meth to cover my one-hundred dollar-a-day habit. Addiction had gripped me hard, continually eating at my self-esteem. Could I ever quit?

The day my life changed forever is vivid. I am so thankful God is a God of "second chances." I know God had his loving arms around me and made me aware He had a plan for me all along.

Around 3:00 AM one morning in May 2008, I checked my email. For me to be awake, "piddling" around this time of the morning was typical.

Someone sent an email with a link to a "YouTube" video called *Cardboard Testimonies*. In this powerful video, I watched men and women, one by one, come onto the stage of a church. Praise music softly played in the background.

Glued to my computer screen, I watched as each person held a single piece of cardboard in front of them. In bold letters, a black marker scribbled words on the front and back of their cardboard.

As I intently watched the video, a beautiful girl with blonde hair, walked onto the stage. She clasped her cardboard sign in front of her chest. She appeared young, maybe in her late twenties or early thirties. My daughter Dawn would have been about the age of this girl at that time.

About twenty people joined her onstage. Watching my computer screen, I was anxious to read what she scribbled on the cardboard she held. One side read, "Was addicted to meth." She flipped the cardboard over. The words were: "*Now addicted to him.*"

The moment I read her cardboard box, I could feel something strange happening to me. A chill followed by a shiver ran down my spine. I must have viewed it ten or more times, tears streaming down my cheeks the whole time. God was trying to tell me something important, and I was finally ready to listen.

Through the tears this early morning, I recognized Jesus held me in His loving arms imploring, "Kim, this is enough. It is over, and I will take you out of this."

It had been some time since I had heard from the Lord. I believed He had moved far from me. The truth was, it wasn't Him who moved; it was me. Once He spoke to me, I knew the steps I had to take.

The girl on the stage in "Cardboard Testimonies" was named Stephanie. I had no idea the church this video was made at was soon going to be the very church I would start attending with my brother Larry. Come to find out, Stephanie's parents participated in this very church as well. I wanted to meet the person, besides Jesus, who saved my life. Stephanie's parents arraigned for her to meet me in person.

The moment I saw Stephanie, we hugged and cried together. We had a common bond. I recounted how grateful I was for her courage to come out on stage to tell her testimony using an old piece of cardboard. She, of course, gave all the glory to God working through her, which saved my life.

The next step was to kick Satan behind me, in the name of Jesus Christ. I cried out to God, "Lord, I admit I am not strong enough to get over this myself, but I know with You, Lord, I can do anything." I believed the prayer I spoke to Him, and I was all in.

The next day, I gathered a few thousand dollars of dope, scales, and all the paraphernalia associated with my meth addiction. After collecting it all, I found a box and dumped it all in. I could see money falling into the box with every sound of the drugs, scales, paraphernalia, and glass pipes jingling as I dropped them in the box.

The cardboard box was twenty-four inches long, twelve inches wide, and eighteen inches deep, big enough to hold my entire collection. Like a mini coffin, I wanted to bury the past. After placing it all in the box, I crumpled old newspapers and filled it tightly to stifle any noise.

Using packing tape to secure the box, I wrapped the box. I buried the box deep amongst all the other garbage in the dumpster until it was out of sight. It took an enormous amount of determination to carry this box to the dumpster, but I knew I had to be all-in for Jesus.

With each step to the dumpster seemed like a hill too hard to climb, but I could feel God's voice telling me, "You can do this, Kim, and I am right here with you." I was stepping out on faith and allowing God to take the lead.

I must admit the next few days were not carefree. But I knew the best way to stay free from my addiction meant to remain a mile away from it. I acknowledged my former drug friends weren't the "right" kind of friends any longer.

I was trying to get away from my addiction, and those types of friends had only one thing in common; to come to me for their next "fix." My well-being was no concern of theirs.

I realized the need to lean on the Lord for strength to help me over this colossal mountain called addiction. Among drug users is a term, "jonesing." Jonesing relates to the feeling of the need to get a fix right now. When this feeling came over me, I would close my eyes and say under my breath, "Jesus, Jesus, Jesus."

Not being a medical expert—and psychiatrists might argue that this could not help. But for me, it gave me the strength to go one more minute, followed by one more hour without meth.

Each minute and hour that passed made me stronger not to look back and pick up the pipe again. With each day that passed, I knew the Lord was beside me, whispering His promise to take me out of this eighteen-year nightmare I had experienced.

The next few days gave me more strength in the following way: As regular buyers of dope called me to purchase some meth, they heard my conviction I had gotten out of that business. Most had a hard time grasping the idea of losing their dealer.

They would lament, "Come on, Barlow! You can't just leave me cold like this. Don't you have just one hit left for me?" I knew I was pleasing God telling those folks, individually, I was out of that business.

One person kept calling me to see if I had changed my mind about quitting. I finally told him sternly to lose my number. I said, "If Jesus tells me I can sell dope again, you will be the first to know." I never heard from him again.

During my addiction, my brother Larry invited me several times to come to church with him. Satan kept me believing I was not worthy enough to enter a church. My mind would race with thoughts like, "God doesn't want a meth-head coming to church."

"You don't want to quit the meth? Remember how much you enjoy it?" I continued to tell Larry the usual, "Thanks, Larry, I will come to church with you someday."

My brother always supported me and never condemned me. I am so grateful for his love for Jesus and how Jesus's love shined through him. Larry's persistence paid off.

I was so excited to call Larry and find out where to meet him at church next Sunday. I did meet him the following Sunday and knew right then what the Lord wanted.

I rededicated my life to Jesus Christ. Jesus was giving me a new lease on life, a second chance, and a feeling of hope. It was the first occasion I felt right at home. And all of this being in the same church where I watched the *Cardboard Testimony* video.

Who we associate with is like a compass. It points to who we are associating with, and a compass never lies. Sin does to our understanding of the Lord's clear direction what a magnet does to the needle of a compass.

If my compass continued to point in the direction of my past, then I would follow.

Yielding to the Lord is an essential part of receiving His instruction. We cannot tolerate sin in our lives and expect to receive His guidance in another.

So here is a simple test to ask ourselves when a decision is unclear. Is Christ to be glorified in this choice, and can we do this in Jesus's name?

If either answer is no, then don't follow this path, because the Holy Spirit is not guiding us there. His leading always aligns with Scripture and brings glory to God. And glory to God was what He had ahead of me next.

Chapter 14

Specific characteristics a meth-user never loses: Some have a constant side-to-side movement of their lower jaw. My residual trait movement includes stretching my fingers of both hands out to the extent of trying to bend them backward. Because I did it so often during my meth-years, it is a habit I haven't broken.

I had been clean for about three months when a dear friend, Marty, and I were having a conversation. He was an installer at the flooring store where we both worked. Noticing my finger stretching, he asked, "Kim, have you ever done meth before?"

Shocked, I didn't know why he was asking me such a thing. I answered, "Yes, but why do you ask?"

He held his hands doing the bend-the-hand backward movement.

I didn't need to answer him verbally. Marty, too, had been a former meth addict, and his mindfulness told him I was also.

I am blessed Marty observed my doing the tell-tale hand movement because it opened the door for him to invite me to a group called, "Celebrate Recovery," a Christian based recovery group meeting weekly in the evening at a church. I agreed to meet Marty at the next meeting.

Celebrate Recovery was another turning point in my life. Being apprehensive about attending my first meeting went away when the meeting started. I witnessed others who have had or who are going through the same recovery process with which had been a part of my life for the last eighteen years. There was no condemnation. I wasn't alone.

The core learning of this group is to know others are experiencing the same difficulties in their life. The methods of how God helped them back on the right road to recovery led me to realize I wasn't alone. I would highly recommend this group to anyone with a habit, hang-up, or addiction.

God's outcome for the Celebrate Recovery group entering my life was more than I could have known. And to think, I once considered getting high on meth was the most super high there could ever be, but I have never felt a high like I have with Jesus Christ.

Being clean about eight months, a dear man who taught the "Celebrate Recovery" group took me aside after a meeting concluded. He informed me the Lord led him to sponsor me on a "Walk To Emmaus" weekend retreat.

I didn't know what a Walk was all about, but I figured if it was going to teach me more about Jesus, then I was all about doing it.

I accepted his invitation and went on my Walk in May of 2009. This experience is an opportunity to feel God's amazing grace and agape love like I have never felt before. During this weekend, I was able to leave a ton of baggage at the cross. This weekend experience was life-changing. It helped me focus on my new dedication to Jesus, enforcing in my heart how God was going to keep me on the right path for Him. He always has a plan.

After my Walk To Emmaus weekend, I started to see many things differently. God showed me how to listen to the words in songs, instead of only the tune. He taught me to gaze at sunrises and sunsets and all the creation He made for you and me. The retreat called Walk To Emmaus was what I needed for the Lord to set me on fire for Him.

The next year, I was asked to participate in working my first Walk To Emmaus on the weekend in June of 2010. Being a considerable honor, this strengthened my faith even stronger. Being asked to work a walk was such a blessing and honor to be on the "other side."

When the men arrive at the retreat site, I observed these men's hearts somewhat hardened, as was mine before my Walk. After all, they had their walls elevated because they have no idea what this weekend has in store for them.

What a blessing it is to watch God tear those walls down and soften these men's hearts. Their "tear dams" become weak by the end of the weekend, and it wasn't from allergies.

After this Walk, a board member asked to me become a board member of "Golden Spread Emmaus," the local governing board of the local Walk To Emmaus group. How honored I became for such a monumental task. Board membership was a two-year term. God was blessing me more and more as I stayed attentive to Him.

It has been a privilege to have worked several Walks from 2010 through 2015. One evening in November 2015, I received a call from the community lay director. He informed me the board of directors nominated me to be the lay director for Walk #252 in August 2016. The Lay Director is one of the highest honors in this organization. A Lay Director is responsible for recruiting seventeen men, some lay-men, and some clergy-men, for working a Walk.

You could say it was my Walk because God and I oversaw putting it all together until the actual weekend retreat. God's hands were in this Walk all along. I was only the "tool" He used to put the Walk-in place.

Being a lay director wasn't an easy task, but the outcome was phenomenal. During this weekend, I saw some fantastic things happen, and many men's lives changed. Only God could have orchestrated this incredible weekend. If you get a chance to go on a Walk, never turn it down. It changes lives forever. As my life was changed that weekend, God continued to change my life for Him. God gave me some miracles that had me looking up and saying, "I know that was You, God. Only God could choreograph the steps He has in store for me next.

Chapter 15

Another occurrence, what many called a miracle happened about two weeks after rededicating my life to the Lord. The Lord kept tugging at my heart, and He wasn't about to let go.

I don't know how the Lord speaks to others, but He kept speaking to me why I needed to have a talk with my brother Larry about what he has meant to me all these years. God kept instilling in my heart; I should express my feelings to Larry how thankful I was for him, and his never giving up on me.

It's easier for me to write my thoughts in a letter than I am telling a person my true feelings to them.

I decided to obey what the Lord was telling me, and I spent a couple of days writing a letter to my brother.

The letter was a heartfelt pouring out to Larry, listing what he meant to me and changing my entire life. How blessed I was, he never gave up and especially for his inviting me to church. I considered him my mentor, and he needed to know all he had done for me my entire life.

Mid-week, I finished the letter. I sealed the envelope and called Larry on the phone. I asked if he could meet at the park near his house on Saturday afternoon. He asked if everything was all right, and I assured him everything was fine. I told him I had something important I needed to talk about with him.

On Saturday, we met at the park. It was late afternoon, and the sun was soon to set in the western sky. We hugged each other and said our hello's and found a picnic table close by to sit. As with most concrete tables, they are not comfortable for any length of time. We sat facing each other across the table, and I could see he had a worried look on his face, probably wondering what I had to say. He looked at me and said he had been worrying I had found out something terrible was happening to me.

Lovingly, Larry said, "What is it you wanted to talk to me about, Kim?" After his question, I handed him the envelope containing the letter I wrote to him.

He opened the letter and started reading. About halfway through the first page, a tear rolled down his cheek. When he got to the end of the message, he stood up and came toward me with his arms open. I met him. We embraced each other in a huge hug. We both had tears streaming down our cheeks. I know a stronger bond existed between us now.

We said our goodbyes, dried our tears, and we left for our homes. Larry and I became one this day, but there was yet another miracle resulting from this meeting.

The miracle of this story has to do with what Larry then did with the letter. He wanted to keep the message in a safe place. When Larry got home, he started thinking, "Where could I put the letter in case I wanted to reread it?"

He had a full bookshelf. "I will place it in a book so that it will be safe," he decided. This way, it won't get wrinkled as it might if left in a drawer somewhere.

Larry opened the book about halfway, inserted the letter, closed the book, and replaced it alongside the other books.

Larry later admitted he had forgotten where he saved the letter in 2008.

Seven years later, in 2015, Larry and my sister-in-law, Mary, were retiring. They were moving closer to her children around the Austin, Texas, area. Not far from Austin, they chose Round Rock as their new home.

My brother and sister-in-law listed their home for sale in Amarillo, which sold quickly.

The time came to start packing and to have a garage sale to rid themselves of their excess belongings for the move.

Some of the items for the garage sale included the books on the bookshelf. And yes, my letter was still in the book. This miracle paperback sold, as did others, so it was long gone.

On January 28, 2016, eight years after the garage sale, I received a private message on my Facebook page. The letter read verbatim: "I recently purchased a used book from Amazon and inside the book was a letter written by a Kim Barlow to his brother Larry. I have searched the Internet in hopes of finding either of you.

The date of the letter is September 5, 2008. If this happens to be the correct Kim Barlow, please let me know, and I will send you the letter." This person also took a snapshot of the letter and included it in the message.

While reading the message, I almost fell out of my chair. This man named Shawn Scott, who found my letter lived in Decatur, Alabama, nine-hundred and sixteen miles from my home in Amarillo, TX!

The stranger who purchased this book at the garage sale sold it to Amazon. I don't know where Amazon is, but it must be a long way from Amarillo.

What happened next is even more bizarre. Shawn happened to be hunting for the very title of this book. He found this used version online at Amazon and purchased this copy. When the book arrived at his home, Shawn opened it and began flipping through the pages. As he did, the letter I'd written Larry seven years earlier tumbled out onto the floor.

Wondering what had fallen out of his book, Shawn reached down to pick it off the floor. While reading this letter, he could read the sincerity of the writer. He knew he needed to do everything in his power to find the owner.

Shawn had been trying to find me through Facebook. He contacted each Kim Barlow till he located me. I wrote him back and told him this was indeed, my letter. He graciously mailed it back to me. I got the impression that only God could replace the letter into my hands. I want to personally thank Shawn for his faithfulness and efforts to find me.

When I called Larry to tell him the good news about finding the letter, he kept repeating, "Wow, wow!" Larry explained he had forgotten over those eight years where he had put the letter. Several times he had wanted to reread it. Telling him this story, he suddenly remembered where he had put my letter.

God still had more miracles to come.

Chapter 16

I want to share another lesson God taught me one day. This time I was with my brother Randy.

On our way home from church, I wanted to stop at a building supply store for a couple of things I needed. Randy and I went in, got the items I needed, and started walking out to get into my car. I parked a reasonable distance out in the parking lot because I hate "door dings."

As Randy and I walked toward my car, I caught out of the corner of my eye, a slightly neglected lady trying to stop us in our path. Before she got to us, I turned to Randy and said quietly to him, "Oh, man, she looks like a panhandler. If she asks me for food instead of money, I would be more than happy to buy her some food." I went on to tell Randy, "Giving them money, I continued, always makes me think they are going to buy drugs."

Now there she was, standing right in front of us. She looked me right in the eyes and said, "Sir, I do not want any money from you." She pointed to a car a couple of rows over and said, "You see the car over there? Inside is my brother and my ten-year-old son." She added, "My father just died, and we are trying to get to Dallas. We only have forty dollars for gas to get us there, and we are starving. All I am asking for Sir is if you could buy us something to eat."

At this moment, I felt like God slapped me in the face. She was one of God's precious creations in need. I looked around and saw a burger place about a half-block away. I said to her, "Follow me there, and I will get you guys something to eat." She said, "Oh, thank you, sir, and God bless you." As I started toward my car, a tear streamed down my cheek. I was ashamed of what I had said to my brother earlier, knowing God's timing is always perfect.

When we arrived at the burger place, I escorted her into the restaurant and led her to the counter. "Order anything you need," and I instructed the cashier I'd take care of the cost.

The lady ordered three meals to go. I paid for the tab and asked if I could sit with her until her order was ready. She had left her brother and son in the car to wait. She agreed.

When we sat at a table, I told her how sorry I was to hear about her dad's passing. She appeared to be about forty years old. I could see by her drawn face she had had a tough life, but also I could read her smile. I knew she was a believer.

While we waited for her order, I asked, "Ma'am, do you know Jesus?"

Her face lit up. "I sure do. Jesus sent me to you." She and I both started to cry.

I then asked, "Would you mind if I prayed for you now?"

She said, "I would love for you to pray for me."

I said a prayer for comfort and traveling mercies.

After the prayer, I reached into my pocket and withdrew two crisp twenties. "To help you on your way to Dallas," I suggested.

She pushed the money to my chest. "You've already done enough," she said.

I explained I felt like God wanted me to help.

When the waitress brought the food to the table, the lady and I stood. We hugged each other, and she returned to her car with her bounty of food.

I see God as so loving and powerful that He takes an interest in the most intimate details of our lives. God loves us so much, there is nothing which escapes His notice, nor is there a concern we have so small for us to bring before Him.

Isn't it comforting to know our Creator holds us and all of creation in the palm of His hands?

If we all cast our problems in a pile, and we saw everyone else's, we'd gladly grab ours back out. God has compassion on all He created, including you. There was still one person who was very distraught about me quitting my drugs.

My meth dealer was very disappointed. I had been one of his money trees. In the past, we went to a well-built storage building in his back yard, where he weighed up my purchase. He never invited me into his home. His storage building was wired for electricity and had heating/air-conditioning for comfort. He had a sofa with a hidden compartment under the cushions where he kept his supply of meth.

His rules required me to give him a call before I came to his home, followed by two-rings on the phone about two blocks from his home to signal I was almost there. I would drive into his paved alley to a gate in his backyard. When he saw it was me, he unlocked a couple of padlocks to let me into the backyard gate. A sidewalk inside the entrance led to the building.

I remember one evening, he unexpectantly changed the rules. This time when I called to purchase meth, he told me to come to his front door.

When I walked to his front door and rang the doorbell, he met me at the door and invited me in. As we walked together, he led me to his dining room table. The table was large by my standards, tall with seating for eight. I sat down at the table with him.

On his dining room table were stacks of hundred-dollar bills. I was startled seeing this amount of cash covered most of the tabletop. I had never seen this much money in my life. Cash stacks were six-inches tall and nestled side-by-side almost four feet long.

I noticed on his end of the table was a 9mm pistol. My dealer asked, "Hey, Kim. Have you ever seen this much money?"

I said, "You don't have to worry about the pistol. I'm keeping my hands to myself."

He smiled, "Well, Kim, this is what $185,000 in cash looks like."

$185,000!

With this kind of money moving through his hands, I realized I was probably a small-time purchaser. So much for my grandiose ideas of importance.

I never understood why he wanted me to see this much money except to make maybe him feel important.

As I think back, having this much cash on hand limits how you can spend it. In this day and time, it is impossible to take a large amount of currency and purchase an automobile or any large ticket item. A business must report a customer using a large sum of money to control money laundering. I never had this much money passing through my hands. Instead, I was barely selling enough to cover my addiction.

It's difficult to remember during my addiction how I once thought getting high on meth was living a great life. But now, I realize the most prominent high is the one with Jesus Christ in my life.

I had some friends who had to quit drugs differently than me. Their addictions stopped when the police arrested them for drug possession. After their court trials, many had to do time in prison. Those who went to jail say it was their "saving grace" as this was going to be the only way they would have ever gotten off meth.

My "saving grace" is thanking God for *not* letting me get caught! I don't believe I would have survived imprisonment. God knew this, and He kept His loving arms tightly around me all along, even when Joe was on his way to kill me.

Chapter 17

Joe was on his way to kill me, not believing when I said I was out of meth. As many times as Joe called informing he was only seconds away from my home, he never called to let me know he had arrived at my house that early morning.

Joe had pulled into my driveway and got out of his car. He began to walk up to the gate about twenty feet from my front door. Each step toward the gate became slower the nearer he came. It was the still of the morning, as Joe made his way toward my gate-latch. As he reached out for it, I was inside my house with my shotgun loaded and ready.

When Joe reached out to touch the latch, he later told me something warned him, "Don't do it." I sat in anticipation for the next few hours, wondering if Joe was coming to my home or not.

Even in Joe's drug-induced state-of-mind, I thank God Joe listened to the hint in his ear this early morning. We both now know God was protecting him and me from each other. God had a plan for us both.

After I had given up dealing with meth, Joe found himself having a tough time. I knew how Joe felt. He would go a couple of days feeling like he could quit, only to convince himself, "One more hit of meth won't hurt me."

Joe's reasoning would put him right back where he was before he stopped. Meth addiction is a helpless feeling. You want to quit, but you can't figure how to do that.

When Joe knew I was off the meth and was no longer selling, we decided to stay in contact with each other periodically. Sometimes, Joe would manage for a week-or-two without meth, and he would stop by my work to visit while he was sober.

When Joe felt compelled to come to see me, many times, he would say, "Kim, there is something different about you. You seem to glow you when I look at you. I wish I could have this, too."

I explained I had turned my life over to Jesus. I asked him to never give up on Jesus too.

Joe eventually went to rehab, is drug-free, and is on fire for the Lord. He is now my accountability partner and my best friend. We have a strong spiritual bond now, closer than any two blood-brothers could experience.

There isn't a time we meet to talk, one or both of us almost always shed a tear. We concur with how great the Lord is and how He blessed us that night.

To think the Lord loved two ole' wretches like us from the horrible times crippled by meth and put us where we are now is pretty amazing.

Joe is now a truck driver and spreads the love of Jesus on his CB radio, traveling the highways of the United States. He tells people all over this land about the night he escaped being shot to death, and about the whisper at the gate one still early morning. Joe shares the story at truck stops, and to anyone and everyone who will listen. He, like me, gives all the credit and honor to our Savior Jesus.

Joe and I have come a long way from where we once were. Still not perfect, but are a work in progress.

Seeing Joe's faith growing, the Lord laid on my heart to sponsor Joe on a Walk To Emmaus. The Walk provided Joe with that giant step he needed to refocus his life on the Lord.

Joe and I frequently talk about our brotherly love for each other. We express how sacred it is to be free from meth. I can honestly say I love this man.

Only God could have orchestrated our outcome. What a sad thing to think, at one time in my life, my thinking included a human being's life meant nothing when it came to drugs.

I will be honest: Breaking my addiction wasn't easy. You must change your entire friend-base if you want to rid yourself of the habit. In my testimony at churches and recovery groups, I add, "If you sleep with skunks, you're gonna smell like skunks."

Joe and I are a deviation from the common rule. God must have a reason for our continued friendship, and I thank Him for this.

If you are struggling with an addiction, you need to know these valuable tools about former friends in the drug culture.

If those old friends were your friends, wouldn't they be trying as hard as they could to get you to stop using drugs? They are your friends only because misery seeks company.

Yielding to the Lord is an essential part of receiving His direction.

God can teach us valuable lessons we didn't think we needed to know. When God leads people to ask me to share my testimony at churches, youth groups, and recovery groups, it is terrific when afterward, a member of the audience invariably comes to me and says, "You know something, Kim? I wondered what led me to be here, and I know it was to hear your testimony. You, sir, have given me new hope." I let them know it is for the glory of God, not me.

My main goal in life would be to teach one more person to realize, trapped in their addiction is not the only way out.

Maybe you or someone you know may be struggling to end an addiction. Dependance isn't exclusive to just drugs. I know people who have horrible cravings of money, work, alcohol, and other material objects.

Now please, don't get me wrong. Rehabs are tremendous and have helped thousands of people. But when people want to know what kind of detox I went through, I tell them, "My Rehab Is Spelled J-e-s-u-s." God has taken me to places I thought I could never go.

Maybe you feel your habits, hurts, and hang-ups are too much for you to handle?

God usually doesn't show us where he is taking us. Like driving a car at night, our headlights never shine to our destination, but just in front of us. Never let this detour us from going toward our goal.

God's Word is like headlights in dark times. His Words will keep us from driving into the ditch of bitterness and despair. His Word promises he will never leave us or forsake us, and He tells us our trials are there to make us better, not bitter.

You won't stumble in the dark if you walk in the light of God's Word. So, the next time you feel as if you are driving in the dark, remember to trust your headlights. God's Word will light your way.

Are you the exception out of billions of people who thinks you aren't significant enough to be singled out knowing God loves you?

You want positive proof God thinks you are special? Jesus Christ died for you. Because of the Father's love for you, He sent His Son to die a brutal death on the cross with you on His mind.

None of us deserve the Father's care and protection, but thankfully, deserving isn't the basis for His love. Don't be distracted by Satan's lying voice and miss the opportunities and love God has for you, yes you.

Past experiences—good and evil have deposited something inside of us. Those challenges have sharpened us to help make us who we are today.

Because God sent His Son to die a brutal death while we were all still sinners, I have to ask, "Why me?" I mean, why would God care about an ole' former meth-head, wretch, and a sinner like me?

The dark and sinful deeds of my past, motivated by a heart even more ominous, and yet God loved me? The truth is, God loves us not because of who we are, but because of Who He is.

Even though I cherished my sin, protected it, and denied its wrongdoing, God still loved me enough to save this ole' wretch, forgive me, and set me free.

It is beyond comprehension when I think, "Why me?" Have you noticed how God has a habit of picking up nobodies and making them somebody?

When the enemy brings hardship into our life, God has a way of taking our experiences and turning it around to our advantage. He will put the right people in our path, the right opportunities, and the right circumstances to move us toward our God-given destiny.

We find ourselves going along with a situation because we don't want to hurt the other person's feelings. Did you feel the Holy Spirit prompting it was wrong?

If we felt wrong, we are compromising the Holy Spirit, who warned us. Small compromises lead to larger ones until finally, our consciences weaken. Satan tempted me to try meth one time, saying, "Go ahead, Kim. It won't hurt you if you snort this in your nose."

Satan had me right where he wanted me. God does not approve compromising or justifications. He does want those who follow Jesus to be strong enough to resist making compromises and develop a strong armor.

We must find the courage to trust in God, even when we are misunderstood, persecuted, or falsely accused. Ultimately, whenever we explore evil, no matter how much we compromise or justify the means, we always lose.

Chapter 18

After rededicating my life to the Lord in May 2008, I have a whole new meaning of my life. I want to please Jesus, not me.

In 2009, I began reading Scripture daily. I joined Facebook and started to put a verse on my page daily. As each day passed, it seemed people were hungry for the Word as the positive comments people would comment about my posts.

By 2010, I would add a few words of my own to the Scripture. Each year I would add more thoughts to the Scripture I was writing. In July of 2017, I decided to open a group page titled, "Real Men and Women Who Follow Jesus." As of this writing, this group has over eleven-thousand members following my post, which I put out every day, seven days a week.

I wanted to share some of these in hopes of encouragement to all who like to start their day off with a positive word.

SENTIMENTS

Have a better view of yourself

> He fell to the ground and heard a voice
> say to him, "Saul, Saul, why do you per-
> secute me?" (Acts 9:4, NIV)

I love how Jesus picked some pretty rough and tough characters to become His disciples. In Acts 9, Ananias saw Saul the Pharisee, who was having people persecuted and even executed. But God told Ananias not to focus on who Saul was but to focus on who he had become.

If you are like me, we sometimes see ourselves only as who we were with all our failures and disobedience, but God sees us as new creations, and who we are becoming through the power of the Holy Spirit. If you are looking and living for your past, it is time you forgave yourself. God certainly has and wants you to become an instrument to whom others wish to what you have, namely Jesus Christ in you.

Today is a brand new day to ask the Lord to help you have a better view of yourself. Heck, if Jesus can save a former meth-head and sinner like me, He certainly will love you too.

Does your shifter cost too much to repair?

"Yet, O Lord, you are our Father. We are
the clay, you are the potter; we are the
work of your hand." (Isaiah 64:8, NIV)

On my sixteenth birthday, my brother Larry gave me
his 1956 Chevy Belair two-door car. It was perfect except
the shifter wasn't working very well. Due to limited funds,
I could not restore it and sold it for $75. This car would
have been the perfect car for restoration and would be worth
thousands of dollars now.

I am so glad that our Potter, Jesus Christ, is in the restoration business. Who among us hasn't felt like a broken or
cracked piece of pottery? We may have been battered and
bruised, but thankfully because the Lord is the God of restoration and forgiveness, if we come to Him humbly, we are
never without hope.

Maybe you feel like your shifter costs too much to
repair? With God by your side, He knows you are so worthy
of repair, that He sent His only Son to die so you could be
perfect in His arms in heaven for eternity.

Is it time for you to quit ignoring where restorations
needed in your life? Give it to Jesus, and you will find safety
in His arms.

A New Preacher in Town

"Then you will know the truth, and the truth will set you free." (John 8:32, NIV)

Several years ago, a preacher from out-of-state accepted a call to a church in Houston, TX.

Some weeks after he arrived, he had to ride the bus from his home to the downtown area. When he sat down, he discovered that the driver had accidentally given him a quarter too much change. As he considered what to do, he thought to himself; *You'd better give the twenty-five cents back.* It would be wrong to keep it.' Then he thought, 'Oh, forget it, it's only a quarter. Who would worry about this little amount anyway, the bus company gets too much fare; they will never miss it. Accept it as a gift from God and keep quiet.'

When his stop came, he paused momentarily at the door, and then he handed the quarter to the driver and said, "Here, you gave me too much change." The driver, with a smile, replied, "Aren't you the new preacher in town?"

"Yes, sir," the preacher replied. The driver said, "Well, I have been thinking a lot lately about going somewhere to worship. I just wanted to see what you would do if I gave you too much change. I'll see you at church on Sunday."

When the preacher stepped off of the bus, he grabbed the nearest light pole, held on, and said, "Oh God, I almost sold your Son for a quarter." Our lives are the only Bible some people will ever read.

As Christians, this is a horrifying example of how much people watch us and will put us to the test. Always be on guard—and remember, we carry the name of Christ on our shoulders when we call ourselves Christians.

What Are You Most Hungry for in Life?

"He who is full loathes honey, but to
the hungry even what tastes bitter tastes
sweet." (Proverbs 27:7, NIV)

When salmon fish return miles upstream to spawn,
bears will be waiting to grab them out of the river, thus gorging
themselves to the point of not being able to take one
more bite.

I see us acting the same way when it comes to how we
use our Spiritual hunger. The lack of inner emptiness will
weaken our discernment as we make decisions. It persuades
us that it's okay to settle for anything that fills us up, even if
it is a sin. God wants so much more for us than a life lived
at the mercy of our hunger. He wants us to be filled with
Christ's love so that everything you do and say passes through
a filter by the name of "Jesus."

What are you most hungry for in life? If you are trying
to "fit-in" with the crowd of bitterness, then that bitterness to
God will make the taste sweet to you.

Jesus, the bread of life in you will never make you hungry. "Father, please help us to focus on You in everything we
say and do." Isn't God's Son worth it?

Our Freedom in Christ

"You have been set free from sin and
have become slaves to righteousness."
(Romans 6:18, NIV)

Before you were a Christian, you were a slave in bondage to sin. Some folks feel burdened because when God saved them, they still were slaves to sin. They have a hard time obligating to honor God in every area of their life to honor God. It is as though it is an option for a Christian to live a righteous life, depending on who we are around.

Honest living is not something we try to do occasionally but is a mandatory obligation for every child of God. Our freedom in Christ is not the freedom to do what we want. It is the freedom to live righteously, something we could not do when we were in bondage to sin.

Now that we are free to live righteously, we must allow the Holy Spirit to produce in us a holy, sanctified life. For me, I would much rather be a slave to righteousness, rather than being bound to sin.

Say No to Sinful Desires

"For physical training is of some value, but godliness has value for all things, holding promise for both present life and the life to come." (1 Timothy 4:8, NIV)

I know many who want self-discipline but struggle to achieve it. They seek health food, supplements, read articles on how to stay healthier, and go to seminars on how to live longer. But look at the verse above again. Notice it wants us to realize all this self-discipline toward our physical well-being is of very little value compared to living a godly life.

Godliness is a Godward attitude that does what pleases the Lord. Discipline for godliness requires that we do reading, studying, and meditating on Scripture a priority. It means we say no to sinful desires and patterns to obey the Lord.

In return, our life will have a mindset transformed into Christlikeness, a clear conscience, and a spirit that is peaceful and joyful.

Our obedience to the Lord extends even further. This earthly life is a mere vapor in time, but godliness goes with us into heaven and leads to eternal rewards of a life lived wholly for Christ. Be sure and take your Christian vitamins: "B1."

What Will Your Eulogy Be at Your Funeral?

"For death is the destiny of every man;
the living should take this to heart."
(Ecclesiastes 7:2b, NIV)

Is someone else going to hold the pen when writing your eulogy at your funeral?

What if every day we were writing a resume of how people we came into contact felt about us? Would they mention us as a loving, forgiving, and kind person, or would they remember us as a gossipping, short-tempered, egotistical person?

It's never too late to develop eulogy virtues and quit playing an actor as to what other people see in us. Paul said, "Follow my example, as I follow the example of Christ." (1 Cor. 11:1, NIV).

We will never go wrong writing the story of our life if it involves Jesus as our model. How much would our lives change if we lived each day with our eulogy in mind? What words will you want the eulogist to speak at your funeral? Right now is the right time for us to pick up the pen and start writing, and telling everyone, you see what Christ has done in your life. That's what matters most.

God Is Right—It Is Right to Give Him Thanks

"But you, O Lord, are exalted forever."
(Psalm 92:8, NIV)

Perhaps you know people who find it easier to complain to others about all they do for the Lord instead of using that energy to praise God for every breath they take? God says it's good to give Him thanks and praise, and obviously, there are huge benefits associated with gratitude, but for whom?

Thanksgiving magnifies the Lord and can affect those who hear us praising and thanking God. Your complaining of all you have to do for God can drive others away, thinking they don't need one more burden in their life. Your complaining takes away God's goodness because you are focusing on you instead of Him.

Praising God will give amazing mental, emotional, and spiritual change when we begin voicing praise for Him.

Recalling our blessings and the many ways God has expressed His goodness reminds others of His faithfulness. Please quit telling me how much you do for God. Instead, tell me of all the goodness He has done in your life. God is right—it is good to give thanks. I will exult you always, my precious Lord.

Are You Fed up with Your Grumbling?

> "Finally, my brothers, rejoice in the
> Lord!" (Phillippians 3:1, NIV)

We all would do well to discover how to face difficult situations with a tranquil, settled spirit rather than with frustration and anxiety.

We need to take a lesson from Paul, who learned to be content in every circumstance, excellent and evil.

I have acquaintances who, on their own, have not been able to say "no" concerning duties at their church. They grumble and chant how they have taken on so many obligations at church; it is affecting their environment around them.

The apostle Paul used situations like these to glorify God, choosing to trust the Savior no matter what.

When you are fed up with your grumbling, disappointment, and dissatisfaction, then you are ready to let the Lord teach you His new way of living. Isn't it time to turn that negative energy into making people hear how the Lord has blessed you?

We will never be able to avoid awkward situations, so why not turn those into people hearing you glorify the Lord? Wise is the person who wants to give honor than receive it.

Many false prophets have gone out in the world.

"Dear friends, do not believe every spirit, but test the spirits to see whether they are from God because many false prophets have gone out in the world." (1 John 4:1, NIV)

John urged his readers to stand against enemies of the faith by using scriptural principles to analyze their words and actions.

Many people think we are living in a world of the "enlightened age." Anyone with an opinion and a platform is welcome to share their version of the truth. Crafty false messages come from places we might not expect.

Just as our beliefs are to impact every facet of our being, so a bit of poison injected into our lives can contaminate areas in our lives. We need to be aware of the type of information and attitudes that enter our minds. A heart full of Scripture will help us recognize an anti-Christ attitude allowing us which to compare it too.

Just as a bank teller goes through training on how to recognize a counterfeit bill, believers will understand and discard an anti-Christ attitude when it reaches their ears.

Give Glory to God

> "And we pray this in order that you may live a life worthy of the Lord and may please him in every way." (Colossians 1:10, NIV)

How do you define gratitude? I describe it as being rescued from one power of destiny to another, death to life.

In Christ, we have been saved and have received the gift of grace. Paul wrote: "For he has rescued us from the dominion of darkness and brought us into the kingdom of the Son he loves, in whom we have redemption, the forgiveness of sins" (Colossians 1:13, NIV).

Reading this, why don't we have more gratitude for being more obedient to our Savior, Jesus. Some believe they have a "free rein" to sin because of God's grace.

Isn't it worth pondering all that being rescued means to us? Being saved from sin, you should be able to help in the rescue of others.

If we find ourselves speaking of all, we do for God, that is the wrong frame of mind. Instead, we should be praising God for all the grace He has provided us.

Fill Your Mind with Scripture

"But there were also false prophets among the people, just as there will be false teachers among you." (2 Peter 2:1, NIV)

I notice people expect those who talk about God must also be serving Him, and His people's best interests.

But sadly, many warnings about deceivers in the church are as pertinent today as when the New Testament writers penned them.

A deceiver attempts to manipulate to exploit his hearers, using half-truths and false promises to draw followers to themselves. Many false teachers will have morality problems.

In the words of Jesus: "See to it that no one misleads you" (Matt. 24:4, NIV). How can you see past a false teacher's camouflage? Fill your mind with Scripture to compare one's words and actions with God's truth. Be cautious of the false teachers among you.

Are You Blind to What God Calls Sin?

> "But mark this: There will be terrible times in the last days." (2 Timothy 3:1, NIV)

If you are like me, have you noticed we could see opposition to Jesus is growing in our culture? I see it in people who commit various sins once condemned are gaining acceptance. These same folks have bought into Satan's lie that we can live without the Lord and still find happiness, prosperity, and peace.

Pride caused Satan cast from heaven, and it prevents people from submitting to Jesus's authority. Adding to all these include abusive behaviors, lack of self-control, and unforgiving attitudes.

Are you blind to what God calls sin? The devil tempted Eve to believe she could find satisfaction outside of God's will, and he is doing the same with us today. Never cave into that liar, Satan. Jesus is much more powerful than him. Satan, I was looking in the back of the Bible, and guess what? In the end, God wins! Isn't it time we put our hope in Jesus's promises?

Come Out Wherever You Are

"And they hid from the Lord God among
the trees of the garden. But the Lord God
called to the man, "Where are you?"
(Genesis 3:8b–9, NIV)

"Peekaboo, I see you." is a saying a child often says while playing hide-and-seek. And yet many adults like to play this game with God. But playing this game with God is more like a game of pretending to hide because no matter what, God sees all our dirty thoughts and wrong choices.

We know when we do wrong, but then we like to justify by pretending He can't see us.

Maybe you feel like you have to hide from the Lord? The good news is; no matter what we did five minutes ago, or five years ago, God wants us to come out of hiding and into a relationship with Him.

"Come out," God is calling to us. "I want to see you, even in your most shameful parts." God loves us unconditionally, so why not come out of hiding, quit our justifying, and let's all get busy for God. God wants to know, "Where are you?"

Today within us, we have the Holy Spirit.

"Come, follow me," Jesus said, "and I
will make you fishers of men." (Matthew
4:19, NIV)

We often refer to ourselves as followers of Christ but fail the test when it comes to our actions and thoughts.

You see, being a Christ-follower is not merely an identification with Him; it's a commitment of obedience that demands to leave behind anything that gets in the way of living fully for Him.

To be a fisher of men requires us to give up all the things that would cause others listening and watching believe we *are* Christ-followers.

Maybe you are a leader in your workplace? What a beautiful battlefield that would be to let those around you see and hear Jesus in you.

Today within us, we have the Holy Spirit, who directs our path and corrects us when we go astray. Never become blind to what God calls sin in our lives. Never let the unfaithfulness of others determine what we do and say.

Don't Be Overcome by Struggles

"But just as he who called you is holy,
so be holy in all you do." (1 Peter 1:15,
NIV)

There is not one person reading this that hasn't experienced challenges in their life.

No matter how hard the circumstances might have been, life has purpose and meaning in Christ. Our heavenly Father has promised always to be with us like a Shephard caring for his sheep. Troubled times can become opportunities for us to learn more about God's faithfulness to draw on His strength.

Satan will encourage us to pursue any path except God's route for holiness. If we find it hard to be holy or set apart, it begins with giving up control over our own life and yielding to the Holy Spirit's authority.

As we submit to Him, He will express the life of Christ through us. Anything short of this is telling God He doesn't know what He is doing. While struggles are a part of everyday life, we don't have to be overcome by them. "Be holy in all you do."

It's Easy to Become Frustrated

"Cover their faces with shame so that
men will seek your name, O Lord."
(Psalm 83:16, NIV)

Recognizing a need in someone's life can be one of the most fabulous invitations from God we will ever experience. But it is also easy to become frustrated by the problems of others. They can overwhelm us as you become aware of the need after need.

When God places people in our life who are in need, He is mindful of what they lack. Rather than looking at each new problem as one more drain on our time and energy, ask God why He placed us in this situation. Maybe some of these people we're trying to reach have become unapproachable due to the repercussion we might face if we speak to them about our concerns?

When those feelings happen in our hearts, immediately go to the Father and say, "Father, you knew this was going to happen. What did you intend to do through me that would help this person become closer to You?"

How Might We Honor God More Fully?

"We are therefore Christ's ambassadors, as though God were making his appeal through us." (2 Corinthians 5:20, NIV)

Integrity: "firm adherence to a code of especially moral or artistic values." I heard a story of a person who drew a "stick-man" on a piece of paper. They then outlined the same stick-man a little wider, saying, "The inner drawing is how I speak around some people, while the outer one is how I speak around others.

The difference between the two drawings represents the measure to which we have integrity. For instance, do the words that proceed from our mouth sound differently around our pastor or a small child, then it does around others? Are the people in our sphere of influence seeing integrity in that?

Notice in the definition of "integrity" above it states, "a firm adherence."

Why can't we see we are Christ's ambassadors, no matter who we are around? How might we honor God even more fully with complete integrity? Isn't Jesus worth it?

Jesus Is My Treasure

"For where your treasure is, there your heart will also be." (Luke 12:34, NIV)

Most Christians are quick to claim that God is their priority. Some find it difficult to talk about their relationship with God, but they can gossip easily about their family and friends.

Some boldly approach strangers to sell a product, yet are painfully timid telling others about their Savior. Some will complain about the hundreds of hours they volunteer at their church but feel like they have no time available to serve God.

What we value most is our wealth, just as our conversations with others determine where our riches are. If we are unsure of our treasures, examine where we spend our time and money.

Ask your friends to tell you what they think is most important to you. It may surprise you to know what others consider to be our treasure. What others know us for is a good indication of what our riches are.

Never let someone mean or negative rent space in your head. Instead, love God and love people and let God sort the others out later. Jesus is my treasure.

The Benefits of Prayer Are Many

"Let not my heart be drawn to what is
evil, to take part in wicked deeds with
men who are evildoers; let me not eat of
their delicacies." (Psalm 141:4, NIV)

Does our devotion to the Lord express itself in a desire
to glorify Him? Do we tend to be drawn to evildoers and
their wicked deeds because we want to fit in?

A solution would be to get serious in our prayer time.
As we spend time talking with our heavenly Father and reading His Word, we'll start to see the world from His divine
perspective.

Things that matter to God will become our concerns
as well, and our prayers will increasingly reflect His interests
and desires. Being in prayer like this naturally has a purifying
effect on us.

The Lord will reveal personal areas of ungodliness, giving us the power to change. The benefits of prayer are many,
but the greatest of all is the joy received from being with the
Lord whom we've grown to know and love.

Today, I pray you will realize the most important one to
please in your life is God, not man. If God is on your mind,
it's because you are on His.

Our Time on Earth Is Temporary

"All the days ordained for me were written in your book before one of them came to be." (Psalm 139:16, NIV)

I have come to some conclusions: *God already knows the duration of each person's life.* No amount of money, vitamins, exercise, plastic surgery, or a diet are going to add one more second or stop that moment. So how can we prepare for what's next?

First, receive Jesus as your Lord and Savior through faith, surrender your life, and strive to walk according to His will.

We must not view this world as your home. When we do that, we will look for security and worth in worldly success, and we won't be able to maintain an eternal perspective.

If you are reading this, there is an inescapable fact that your time on earth is temporary. Wouldn't it be foolish to not prepare for something so inevitable? Feeling grieved into depression is not the time to clam-up and get farther from God. Instead, it would behoove us to get back to a good church.

Getting into God's Word will strengthen our faith.

Are You Practicing Religion?

"Come to me, all you who are weary
and burdened, and I will give you rest."
(Matthew 11:28, NIV)

Do you find yourself or know someone that proclaims Christianity exhausts them draining their energy? The probability is they are practicing religion instead of enjoying a relationship with Jesus Christ.

When I think serving God is all up to me, I'll notice I have begun working for Him instead of walking with Him. The difference is, If I'm not walking with Christ, my spirit becomes dry and weak. It feels like nothing seems right. Even people can become annoyances instead of fellow humans created in God's image.

Do you feel like you are practicing religion instead of enjoying a relationship with Jesus? Lay down your burden, and Jesus will give you rest.

Here is a great explanation: Religion is a man sitting in church thinking about fishing. A relationship is a man fishing thinking about God. If you are weak and burdened, God will give you rest.

We want to make Christ attractive to all.

"Therefore, since Christ suffered in his
body, arm yourselves also with the same
attitude." (1 Peter 4:1, NIV)

Pondering on today's passage reminds us we are engaged in a battle to arm ourselves with the same attitude Christ had in His suffering.

Jesus willingly submitted to the Father's will and died a brutal death on a cross while you and I were on His mind. His sacrifice meant He also wanted us to break any attachment to our previous sins.

When we accepted Jesus as our Savior, it requires us to live differently from the world around us. Our lifestyle should be that everyone will see and hear Jesus in our being.

Others will find this offensive because it exposes their sin. They may respond by smearing us in an attempt to make themselves feel better.

We all want to make Christ attractive to all, but in reality, we may make others uncomfortable. God never intends for suffering to defeat us. Instead, His purpose is to make us a powerful witness for Christ.

God Intended It for Good

"You intended to harm me, but God intended it for good." (Genesis 50:20, NIV)

We all have suffered pain and injustice at the hands of others. Conflict, mistreatment, and criticism are a few we may endure. But how we react is a lesson in grace and holiness.

The Lord doesn't want us to focus on the wrongs done to us. Instead, He wants us to keep our eyes fixed on Him. When reading God's Word, He will reveal His ways and purposes as He guides us through the suffering times. His indwelling Holy Spirit enables us to respond godly by forgiving those who wrong us.

The pain we carry in our life can be used for good if we'll forgive our offenders and trust the Lord's ways. "You intended to harm me, but God intended it for good." Isn't this true in our life also? Are we growing more or less like Christ as a result?

God Is Ready to Pardon You.

> "Shouldn't you have had mercy on your
> fellow servant just as I had on you?"
> (Matthew 18:33, NIV)

Mercy is an underserved gift for every sinner reading this. The merciful person does not demand justice for the guilty person.

Have we considered the incredible, undeserved mercy granted to us all? Could any offense another commits against us be as undeserved as the abuse hurled against the sinless Jesus on the cross?

How quickly we forget the undeserved mercy, God graciously bestowed on us, only to focus on the injustices we endure from others.

If we find it difficult to forgive others, we may need to think back where we were the first time God forgave a sinner like us.

You not forgiving someone is like keeping a prisoner inside. And that prisoner is you.

A Red Warning Light Is On

"Serve whole-heartedly, as if you were serving the Lord." (Ephesians 6:7, NIV)

A wife phoned her husband, explaining her auto engine seemed to lock-up all of a sudden.

The man asked her if any warning light had come on in the dash? She said the little red "oil-can" symbol did. Frustrated, the man told her that was the oil light, and she was out of oil in the engine.

"Why didn't you stop when the light came on," he exclaimed? She replied, "I thought it would get bright red when I needed to turn it off!"

Is this how we treat the "red-warning" lights from sin? Justifying why we sin is like the woman ignoring her dash light coming on.

God doesn't want to hear our excuses and justification why we sin; He wants to know why we continue to ignore the warning lights He gave us in our owner's manual, the Bible.

The good works we brag about will neither satisfy divine justice nor pay for our transgressions. After sending Jesus to us and dying a brutal death on the cross, God would like to know why we don't consider that good enough for us to live in righteousness? If your red light burning bright red, ask God to fill your reservoir with His Word.

What Is Hindering Your Progress?

"Be imitators of God, therefore, as dearly
loved children." (Ephesians 5:1, NIV)

What are those in our sphere of influence hearing when they are around us?

As Christians, our calling is to a high moral standard, yet we may feel as if we're failing more than succeeding. Perhaps our language isn't as pure as we know it should be, or we haven't overcome some of our bad habits.

We can become discouraged when we don't understand what is hindering our progress. It's a mind thing because the way we reason affects how we act. We can't expect ever to change if we justify our disobedience. Filling our minds with the truth of God's Word will ensure we are counteracting those justifications.

If we associate with people who don't share our standards, the temptation will turn to compromise. Are you being influenced by friends, television, or social media more than you are by the Word of God? As we put your trust in our Creator, ask Him to replace wrong thoughts with godly ones, and our behavior will transform to be like Christ.

God Is There during the Bad Times Too

"For we do not preach ourselves, but Jesus Christ as Lord, and ourselves as your servants for Jesus's sake." (2 Corinthians 4:5, NIV)

Adversity has a way of wearing us down, moving from one problem to the next without a pause in between. How we respond to hardship reveals our real character and our knowledge of God.

"I trust in God" is easy to say in hard times, but we must recognize God is there in the bad times too. Surrendering is essential to make it through hardships.

Every trial is a chance for the light of Christ to shine through us. It is also a means He uses to mature our faith, conform us to the likeness of His Son, and fulfill His unique plan for our life.

Momentary afflictions produce for us "an eternal weight of glory far beyond all comparison (v. 17). When we trust in the Lord's faithfulness, we'll choose to focus on Him to bring us through. Maybe it's time to let go and let God?

Vengeance Is God's Responsibility

> "Make every effort to live in peace with all men and to be holy; without holiness, no one will see the Lord." (Hebrews 12:14, NIV)

An unforgiving spirit is like you drinking rat poison daily, expecting the other person will die.

We resist offering forgiveness, thinking that a pardon excuses the wrongdoer. True forgiveness means letting go of the offense with the knowledge that vengeance is God's responsibility, not ours.

Stubbornly refusing to forgive may seem like a way to get even, but it hampers our ability to enjoy life and erodes our fellowship with the Lord. An unforgiving spirit hinders our ability to love, poisoning the atmosphere in homes and workplaces.

Vengeance is God's responsibility, not yours. Let God be God.

God Never Made Any Junk, Including You

"Yet to all who received him, to those who believed in his name, he gave the right to become children of God." (John 1:12, NIV)

Do you get the feeling sometimes? *Does God care about me?* We know from the Bible that "God is love," which means His very nature characterized compassion and concern. Our model Jesus is our most exceptional example of how to express love.

The next time you feel like God doesn't care about you, I want you to remember how God gave the supreme demonstration of His love at the cross. No one reading this, being dead in our sins, deserved Christ going to the most considerable length possible to give us life.

The Son of God came to earth as an expression of His Father's awesome, fathomless, infinite love and did for us what no one else could do. All the while, you were on His mind!

Remember Jesus's own words on this subject: "Greater love has no one than this, that one lay down his life for his friends." (John 15:13, NIV)

God is holy, means He is perfect in His love—He'll never make a mistake in the way He loves us. God never made any junk, and that includes you.

Peace and Joy Can't Co-Exist

"A hot-tempered man must pay the penalty." (Proverbs 19:19, NIV)

Anger is a common emotion when we encounter threats,
injustices, frustrations, and insults. Too often, we respond
unjustly by holding on until it becomes part of our character.

There, it starts to agitate emotions and twist our thought
process. Peace and joy can't coexist with the anxiety and frustration that accompany bitterness.

Then, poisoning the character, anger spills over and
affects others. We might throw flaming arrows, hurting even
those who weren't the cause of the rage. And sadly, we raise
shields of protection to protect ourselves, leading to stressed
relationships and isolation.

If people are having to "walk on eggshells" around you,
it's most tragic consequence is a broken relationship with
God. He desires to cover His children with blessings, but
angry attitudes cannot receive His riches of character and
calling.

Anger can be so profoundly seated within your soul,
will affect every area of your life.

Ask God to reveal any hidden resentment. Then release
it and take hold of the riches of Christ. "A hot-tempered man
must pay the penalty."

Do Barbers Exist?

A man went to a barbershop to have his hair cut and his beard trimmed.

As the barber began to work, they began to have a good conversation. They talked about so many things and various subjects. When they eventually touched on the subject of God, the barber said: "I don't believe that God exists."

"Why do you say that?" asked the customer.

"Well, you have to go out in the street to realize that God doesn't exist, like why would there be so many sick people? Why so many abandoned children? If God existed, there would be neither suffering nor pain. I can't imagine a loving God who would allow all of these things."

The customer thought for a moment but didn't respond because he didn't want to start an argument. The barber finished his job, and the customer left the shop. Just after he left the barbershop, he saw a man in the street with long, stringy, dirty hair and an untrimmed beard.

The customer turned back and entered the barbershop again, and he said to the barber: "You know what? Barbers do not exist."

"How can you say that?" asked the surprised barber. "I am here, and I am a barber. And I just worked on you!"

"No!" the customer exclaimed. "Barbers don't exist because if they did, there would be no people with dirty long hair and untrimmed beards, like that man outside."

"Ah, but barbers do exist!" answered the barber. "What happens, people do not come to me."

"Exactly!" affirmed the customer. "That's the point! God, too, does exist! People don't go to Him and do not look for Him. That's why there are so much pain and suffering in the world."

Obedience Is to Be a Constant Lifestyle

"Blessed are all who fear the Lord, who walk in obedience to him." (Psalm 128:1, NIV)

Does your godly influence flow from your strong beliefs based on Scripture to all you come into contact with?

Following God doesn't mean living out biblical principles only when it's convenient or comfortable. Obedience is to be our consistent lifestyle, no matter what the circumstances are.

Without that commitment to compliance, we'll waiver back and forth, being a poor witness and eventually give into temptation. God wants to use each of us to impact others for Christ in whatever sphere of influence He has given us.

Wouldn't it be this very moment in your life to commit to God's Word and to trust the Lord with the outcome? Instead of making excuses, why we can't be obedient, let us take that energy toward impacting others that they will see and hear Christ in us. God has a hard time blessing who you are pretending to be.

Take Up the Cross of Christ

"My food," said Jesus, "is to do the will of him who sent me and to finish his work." (John 4:34, NIV)

We, humans, are an independent species. We want things our way, in our time, and on our terms. But Jesus said that anyone who wants to follow Him must deny him-or herself.

Yes, that means we must decline good things because they don't pass the filters' of God's plan. Sometimes following the Lord involves suffering.

What bystanders can't see or experience is the deep satisfaction we gain from doing what is right. Just as the food is to the body, so obedience is to the soul and spirit, honoring God will bring much more pleasure to us at the end of the day.

Even when self-denial hurts, obeying, God brings joy. If we follow Christ, and we prioritize submission to Him, we will know what this devotional is speaking.

What a day it will when we hear, "Well done, good and faithful servant!" If we draw close to the Lord, we will sense His approval. Isn't it time we deny ourselves and take up the cross for Christ?

I am laying a foundation in the word.

"Teach us to number our days aright, that we may gain a heart of wisdom." (Psalm 90:12, NIV)

If you found out you were going to die tomorrow, would you be kinder, love harder, or be more forgiving? I can give us the best Las Vegas odds; One-thousand out of one-thousand reading this right now will die one day.

We recognize that many of the things we do in life require preparation. But do we approach our spiritual life with the same vision, or do we tend to take a casual approach? Do we spend time each day with the Lord in prayer and His Word, or seek Him only when we have a problem?

Imagine you got married but never went home? Your relationship wouldn't be convincing, and likewise, it's doubtful you will have a relationship with God unless we put effort into spending valuable time in prayer and reflection.

These are occasions for strengthening our faith, growing in love for Christ, and laying a foundation in the Word. With something so inevitable as death, why not start this very second to begin to follow in the model God sent us named Jesus?

You May Have Done Too Much

"Do not be deceived: God cannot be mocked. A man reaps what he sows." (Galatians 6:7, NIV)

Do you remember times when God spoke to you, but you gradually realize you've not heard His voice for a long time? God's silence may be hardly noticeable at first.

If you recognize this immediately, seek the Lord and ask Him what adjustments your life requires so you can once again enjoy fellowship with Him.

It may be that we disobeyed His last instructions to us, or He is waiting on our obedience before giving us a new direction. It may include we have unconfessed sin in our life or that we have a damaged relationship.

You may have done too much talking in your prayer times and that He wants you to listen. God's silences can be great times for Him to communicate with you.

Because He is God when He speaks, He expects a listening ear and an enthusiastic response. God will not be mocked!

If we seek Him, He will be found by us; but if we forsake Him, He will leave us.

Is This Where Satan Wants Us to Be?

> "There is nothing concealed that will not
> be disclosed or hidden that will not be
> made known." (Luke 12:2, NIV)

At times the desire for acceptance can tempt us to manipulate people and circumstances. And the fear of conflict can result in compromised standards, as many try to fit in to avoid arguments.

Many times we will use deception out of selfishness to obtain something we want. Even those close to us may think we don't see the trick, but God sees. Those guilty feelings in your conscience God uses so we might confess our sin and turn from it.

Justifying our behavior and continuing in unrighteousness, self-protection will take over. Is this where Satan loves us to be?

Over time, we will even draw away from certain people, so they don't discover our ungodly behavior. If habitual sin builds over time, it can lead to severe consequences, like a damaged friendship, or a broken family. When the Holy Spirit convicts us of ungodliness, do we try to justify and persist in our conduct? It is never wise to argue with someone who believes their lies.

I used to know everything.

> "How much better to get wisdom than
> gold, to choose understanding rather
> than silver!" (Proverbs 16:16, NIV)

During a sermon at church recently, this keeps resounding in my mind: "When an old man is dying, it is if a whole library is burning" (Amadou Hampate).

I reflected this while at my grand-daughters twentieth birthday party. I looked at my granddaughter, remembering when I was twenty and knew it all! Now in my last years of life, I know just how much I didn't know then.

Some of the wisdom God has provided to me over these years means so much more to me now. Knowing God is in charge, His grace is eternal, and the faith He has instilled in me to go on are just a few of the undeserved gifts He provided to me.

Just as our human relationships fall apart without regular contact, so does our intimacy with the Father weakens when we do not spend time with Him. Walking with God is not an impossible mission, but it does require careful attention to the details of your Christian life. Isn't it time you commit to the Lord?

Respect Is One of the Highest Expressions of Love

"For it is God's will that by doing good you should silence the ignorant talk of foolish men." (1 Peter 2:15, NIV)

We have many people watching us as a Christian. That's a good thing to remember as we interact with people at work or with others.

How we respond to difficulties and temptations is a witness for Christianity, and the last thing we want to do is misrepresent Christ. Being equipped for Christlikeness and our witness will be made more accessible, like knowing Scripture will help you view situations from God's perspective, learning how He would respond.

Praying about our problems and bringing our concerns to God will guard our hearts and minds. Prayer is a powerful witnessing tool to a watching world.

Don't let your troubles erupt into anger and blame. Small acts of kindness and a forgiving spirit are a tremendous witness in a world where such things are rare. Aggravations and problems seem like hindrances to us, but our response can change someone's like if it reflects the love of Jesus Christ. Respect is one of the highest expressions of love.

Are you a spectator?

"Never be lacking in zeal, but keep your spiritual fervor, serving the Lord." (Romans 12:11, NIV)

The church is a place for participants, not spectators. Unfortunately, many Christians today think this kind of involvement in others' lives is too personal. So they come on Sunday, stand to sing, sit to listen, then walk out to get back to their own lives.

Many churches have many observant attendees who sit in the pews each week but never touch a fellow Christian's life. Many think *It's just too personal to talk to someone about Jesus!*

Really? If every person on the planet thought like you, we would be one generation from no one knowing Jesus. We are called the body of Christ, and as such, our lives are meant to intersect, touch, and connect with other Christ-followers.

What about you? Are you a spectator seeking what you can get or a participant looking for ways to share Jesus with someone else? Isn't it time you shared Jesus with someone in this hurting world? He is counting on you.

Our Creator Has Given Us His Holy Spirit

> "For prophecy never had its origin in the human will, but prophets, though human, spoke from God as they were carried along by the Holy Spirit." (2 Peter 1:21, NIV)

How important is your Bible to you? The number we own has no measure of their value to us. It's what we do with God's Word and what it does in our heart that reveals how much we treasure it.

There is no argument the Bible is the essential book in the world because it's the only one that is the inspired Word of God. Nothing else ever written can match the wisdom and revelation of the Scripture, period.

Not from Allah, Budda, even the book of Mormon was not God-breathed. The same God who created the universe divinely inspired the writing of Scripture.

Almighty God did so to reveal Himself to us and to explain how sinful humanity can be made right with a holy God. Our Creator has given us His Holy Spirit so we can know His mind through the Bible. However, if we rarely open it, we won't know His thoughts and will lose His blessings and wisdom.

No One Is Born an Atheist

"Although they claimed to be wise, they
became fools." (Romans 1:22, NIV)

I often have admired the faith of an Atheist because
no one is born an Atheist or Agnostic. The Father has given
every person an inborn witness of God's existence, but this
isn't the only evidence offered to humankind.

Creation itself testifies to God's invisible properties,
eternal power, and divine nature. Every person has a free will
to ignore or reject both the infinite and external witnesses
of God. A person who rejects God has a mind that becomes
progressively darker until it can no longer see the light of
truth.

Interestingly, tribes, when found in a jungle who have
never seen any outside influence, are found to be worshiping
something. These tribes understand nothing could be created
by nothing.

Each of us should take the opportunity to share the gospel with people in our sphere of influence. That is God's plan
for the unreached. Is that what others are seeing and hearing
from you? You may be the only Bible someone reads.

Are we treating sin as a credit card?

> "Whoever serves me must follow me;
> and where I am, my servant also will be.
> My Father will honor the one who serves
> me." (John 12:26, NIV)

A seed never planted will not produce a crop. Some refuse to let others see and hear Jesus coming from their being. It's as though we think it's too personal to act as a follower of Jesus.

The underlying problem involves dying to self and broken of our pride and self-sufficiency that we become fruitful and useful to the Lord. Doing this makes us like a single, unbroken grain of wheat remaining unproductive.

With so much at stake, why do we hang on to our short-sighted desires, thus stunting our spiritual growth? Never be distracted by short-term happiness. That isn't the road to maturity that God has prepared for us.

An abundance of God's blessings awaits us if we'll release our grip and let Him do whatever it takes to get us there. Sin is like a credit card. Sin now and pay later.

God Wants Us to Regard His Holiness

"Just as Moses lifted up the snake in the desert, so the Son of Man must be lifted up." (John 3:14, NIV)

Imagine if our lives were like a ladder that we climbed until we die. It would be odd if we stopped part of the way up, and never moved again. Even worse, what if we placed our ladder against the wrong wall after a lifetime of climbing to discover that we had wasted all the years given to us?

Many have to be emptied of all their self-accomplishments and pride to be able to see the need for a Savior. Where have we placed our ladder?

Has God spilled you so you can start climbing again, or are you still bragging about all your "good deeds?" No good works or religious service will never get us into heaven.

But there is something we can believe. God wants us to regard His holiness and realize how far we are from His perfect standard. Then, if we come broken and repentant to Jesus, believing His death paid our debt, we'll become born again and will someday see the kingdom of heaven. Stop fighting it, because Jesus wants nothing from you. He instead wants you.

Our Lives Have a Profound Effect on Those around Us

"As obedient children, do not conform to the evil desires you had when you lived in ignorance." (1 Peter 1:14, NIV)

The dictionary defines accountability as: "an obligation or willingness to accept responsibility or to account for one's actions."

Our life has a profound influence on those around us, including our spouses, children, co-workers, and our friends. I see some who act like the world tries to persuade them to follow it's standard.

With all our Savior, Jesus sacrificed for us; our lives should stand in stark contrast as an example of a righteous person. Our experience should convince those around us of the wisdom of following God.

Never underestimate the positive effect that your obedience will have upon those around you. Our Accountability Partner is Jesus. Do you feel an obligation or willingness to accept responsibility or to account for your actions to Jesus? He is counting on you!

Thank the Lord for the Christ-centered people in your life.

"Because your love is better than life, my lips will glorify you." (Psalm 63:3, NIV)

Have you noticed how sometimes when we're not listening for the Lord's voice, He may send a message through someone else? Maybe it is through a fellow follower of Christ who will advise you about the wrong direction you have been moving recently?

When we're going off course, the heavenly Father will sometimes speak through other believers to reach us. Allowing this is vital to maintain a close network of men and women who love and seek Jesus in their own lives.

Thank the Lord for the Christ-centered people in our life, and pray for wisdom in discerning their counsel. They may be trying to open our eyes to the things we are doing, which God calls sin. Our partial obedience to our Savior is disobedience in His eyes

God Gave Us Two Ears and One Mouth

"The way of a fool seems right to him, but a wise man listens to advice." (Proverbs 12:15, NIV)

One of my favorite thoughts is: *Just because I don't agree with you doesn't make you right.*

Many times it's natural to turn to friends for advice when facing a challenging situation. However, we must always be careful to examine the information offered to us. The counsel may seem sound, but if it's inconsistent with God's Word in any way, we should politely disregard it.

I see in others who tend to heed the advice they want to hear but pass over the real truth of a Scripture that applies. We must distinguish between our fleshly desires and biblical truth. Wise counsel is always consistent with Scripture and points us to God's desires and ways.

The next time we seek an opinion from friends, remember it's still better to trust in the Bible and God's wisdom for guidance.

God gave us two ears and one mouth. We should do twice the listening as we do speaking. "The way of a fool seems right to him, but a wise man listens to advise."

Start Living for the One Who Saved Us

"So, because you are lukewarm—neither
hot nor cold—I am about to spit you out
of my mouth." (Revelation 3:16, NIV)

No one said it would be easy to follow Jesus. Living for God has great rewards when facing temptations.

If we follow our model, Jesus, He will reveal the eternal rewards for loving Him and following Him obediently. Each act of obedience to the Lord is like Him giving us a crown that we will put down at the feet of Jesus one day.

Temptations are unavoidable in this life, but how we react to such adversity is what God wants to know about us. Will we join in, or will we respect that our Savior is more important than our earthly desires?

Take heart. Much Spiritual growth can happen during adversity. But first, we must take our selfish ambitions out of the equation and start living for the One who saved us, gifted us, and equipped us. Never be passive being lukewarm for Jesus.

Ask God to Discipline Your Mouth

"What goes into a man's mouth does not
make him unclean, but what comes out
of his mouth, that is what makes him
unclean." (Matthew 15:11, NIV)

Do we often regret our words? Are there people even
now who are hurt or angry because of things we have said?
Do we tend to gossip or tend to criticize others? Does our
mouth spew grumbling, complaints, or foul words?

These words come from a heart that is unlike God's
heart. One might say, "Oh, but that's just the way I am. I'm
better than I used to be."

Scripture clearly states that an abusive tongue is not
under the control of the Spirit (James 3:3–10). A Scriptural
mouth is a beautiful instrument for the Lord. A heart like the
Father's heart will produce only pure and loving words.

Without making any excuses for our words, ask God to
discipline our mouth so that every word we speak is used by
Him to encourage and teach others.

Knowing we wouldn't act that way in front of our pastor tells me we know better. Your pastor is healthy, but the
very ones who are the sickest are the very ones who need to
hear and see Jesus coming from our being. What comes out
of the mouth, that is what makes him unclean.

Our God Is Not Unsympathetic

"In fact, though by this time you ought
to be teachers, you need someone to teach
you the elementary truths of God's word
all over again." (Hebrews 5:12, NIV)

God, out of His love, has done everything necessary for us to overcome the temptations we face. Because God has revealed to us in Scripture means we will never be confused about the right thing to do.

Even more, He has placed the Holy Spirit within us to guide us in our decisions and to convict us when we make the wrong choices. As if that isn't sufficient to honor Him, the very Son of God humbled Himself, taking all the limitations of frail human flesh, and tempted in every way that we are.

Why is it so hard for us to turn to Jesus when we are feeling tempted? Our God is not unsympathetic and unconcerned with our struggles. God wants us to approach His Son Jesus with confidence, knowing He understands our plight to live righteously.

What is keeping us from asking Christ to help? He alone knows how to aid us when we become tempted.

Allow His Word to Light Our Paths

"He does not know where he is going,
because the darkness has blinded him."
(1 John 2:11b, NIV)

Did you realize if you say something, then add the word "but" means everything I just said means nothing. For instance, "I wouldn't act that way around others, "but" I don't want them to think I fit in."

Fitting in is precisely where that liar Satan wants us. He wants his darkness to blind us with our justifications after the word "but."

I promise you this. Living aligned to God by allowing His Word to light our paths keeps us from living blind. The results will make it where we never have to say, "but" because our words and our actions will match up.

Which would we rather have those around us seeing and hearing from you? It doesn't mean people will have the impression of us knowing everywhere we are going, but rather being someone that knows Who they're following. This very second would be a great time to take the darkness that is blinding you and let Jesus be your Light.

Real Joy Comes from Knowing God

"About midnight Paul and Silas were praying and singing hymns to God, and the other prisoners were listening to them." (Acts 16:25, NIV)

What do people hear and see coming from you? Our joy as a Christian should not depend on our circumstances. It should be different.

You know, we as Christians will always be under a microscope. Especially at work, at church, and home. Real joy comes from knowing God Himself lives within you and has fellowship with you, regardless of who you are around.

The good news is; The more we become like Jesus Christ, and we conform to His will and likeness, the more we realize the remarkable nature of God and how much more we will please Him, not humanity.

Our salvation to others should reflect an ever-increasing miracle in us.

With all, we have to be thankful for should be an ever-increasing desire to guard our hearts against the temptations of the devil because our salvation is so precious to us. The fact is, we cannot fathom such mercy, but it is real nonetheless.

What Do People See in You?

"Since you are precious and honored in my sight, and because I love you." (Isaiah 43:4, NIV)

Do you have an image of yourself that you want others to have of you? It could be your success or godliness, but you will go to great lengths to conceal your "ugly" sides.

Deep down, you may fear you won't be loved if the real you is known. But not with God. Despite your sins and shortcomings, God still loves you immeasurably. When this truth sinks in, it will make you understand that it is more critical everything you do is acceptable to God, and it will make the approval of others less significant.

Being obedient is far more important to God than wearing a mask and trying to "fit in" around others. Because of God's deep love for you, it means you can be real with others. What is the image you portray to others around you? I pray it is Jesus.

Flattery Is Not Eternal

"Blessed are those who are persecuted because of righteousness, for theirs is the kingdom of heaven." (Matthew 5:10, NIV)

God is obvious in His Word that incredible benefits await believers who obey and bring glory to Him. God sees our Spirit-led decisions and actions as worthy of reward.

You may feel unimportant or unessential in this big world, but your every action and word matters to God. Yielding to the Holy Spirit's direction is what God values most.

He also looks at our motivation. Sometimes good works are done for the wrong reasons. When a person seeks the applause of men, their "pat on the back" is their sole reward. While this may feel good at the time, flattery is not eternal.

For me, I know that one day, I'll shed tears of regret over the righteous acts I neglected or the work I did for personal glory.

Do you stop and think how much more you could do for the Lord, or is your selfish self-centeredness holding you back? Jesus is counting on you.

Our Goal Isn't Merely to Resist Temptation

"And that they will come to their senses
and escape from the trap of the devil,
who has taken them captive to do his
will." (2 Timothy 2:26, NIV)

Do you have a sin you want to overcome, but as temptation comes, your willpower erases? Those types of attractions are what causes us the most significant struggles, but sometimes part of the problem is our lack of boundaries.

We are taking steps to protect ourselves, namely by establishing limitations to guard us against wandering into a danger zone. Our goal isn't merely to resist temptation but to move as far possible in the opposite direction, toward godliness.

Trying to withstand temptation is useless unless we first commit to living obediently before God. Submitting to God comes the power to resist.

God warned if we toy with or let our cravings and self-centeredness in the way of temptations, we will fall. If you concentrate on drawing nearer to God, you will escape the traps of the devil. If you honor God, He will honor you.

Who Needs to See Jesus in Us?

"For sin shall not be your master, because you are not under the law, but under grace." (Romans 6:14, NIV)

In our fallen, broken world, all of us are sinners with our collection of weaknesses. The problem is we might keep sinning even when we know the Lord doesn't approve of them. Denying our sins and hiding them, challenges us to think Jesus's power to work within us is impossible.

Jesus taught us differently, though. Jesus told Paul, "My power is made perfect in weaknesses." Our immature, self-centered belief that we can sin-away because of God's grace is not what the Lord wants or expects from us. The very ones who need to see Jesus in us get a different view when we indulge in our sins.

Maybe you are a leader in your church, or are over people at your workplace? Isn't it time you invited Jesus totally into your life and show those who need to see and hear Jesus around you, how obedience from sin you are? It will empress them more than your disobedience to the One who sacrificed His life for us. Father, please forgive us when we act blind to what you call sin. Amen.

His Truth Should Be Enough.

"Indeed, the water I give him will become in him a spring of living water." (John 4:14, NIV)

One of my favorite stories in the Bible for me is the woman at the well. Jesus, who was ideally qualified to condemn people for their sin, didn't crush the Samaritan woman. Instead, He gently critiqued her life with a handful of words.

The results pointed out how her search for satisfaction had selfishly led her to sin. Jesus revealed Himself as the only source of eternal comfort.

Grace and truth, which Jesus used in this situation, are what we should experience in our relationship with Him. And what about you? Isn't it time you invite Jesus to show you areas of your life where you need to grow and become more like Him?

His truth should be enough to prevent us from thinking our sin isn't a serious matter. How is Jesus using grace and truth in your life? Is the Holy Spirit making you aware of where He might want to make changes to honor Him?

Unless you know the very minute you will see Jesus, now would be the perfect second to start accepting our Father in heaven for all the grace He has shown us all. Would you agree?

Are You in for Jesus?

"So, because you are lukewarm—neither
hot nor cold—I am about to spit you out
of my mouth." (Revelation 3:16, NIV)

Have you noticed how some Christians multiply in
their Christian faith while others remain unchanged year
after year?

Jesus was evident in the Scripture above. He wants us all
to be very intentional about our Christianity. That requires
us to experience the fullness of God in every area of our
Christian life and never settle for a shallow, justifying, lacka-
daisical relationship with almighty God.

I see some who will spew filth out of their mouths in
front of some, but not one bad word will come from their
mouth in front of others, proving they know better. Jesus
calls this immature and self-centeredness to be "lukewarm"
toward Him.

Why do some Christians continue to grow in their faith
while others are still lukewarm? Our Christian maturity is
deeply affected by knowing the sacrifice God gave by sending His only begotten Son to die a brutal death all while you
were on His mind. Careful, with your justifications, He is
getting ready to spit you out of His mouth!

Partial Obedience Is Disobedience

"Be imitators of God, therefore, as dearly
loved children." (Ephesians 5:1, NIV)

A young man was behind an older man who was driving slower than he was. The young man became frustrated and couldn't wait to get up beside the older man to honk his horn and show his "IQ" finger to the older man.

Finally, the young man moved beside the older man's car, honks, and shows his "IQ" finger to him.

The young guy was shocked when he noticed it was the pastor at his church, driving the slower car.

Jesus taught each of us that how we treat strangers reflects our relationship with Him. When someone insults us or we hurt one another, the One who loves us takes it personally.

Partial obedience is disobedience in His eyes, and no sin is worth being outside His will. Father, forgive us when we act like You are not present when we act out in our moments of need, anger, and hurt. Amen. Love God, and love people, then everything else will fall into place.

The Sick Ones Need to Hear
Jesus Coming from You

"The deeds of faithless men I hate; they
will not cling to me." (Psalm 101:3b, NIV)

If Jesus were standing next to you, would you spew dozens of profound words at Him? Of course not, but some do it in front of those who need to hear Jesus from their mouth more than anything.

Do we believe Jesus will compromise our justifications using foul words? Even though our reason for partial obedience may sound logical, our arguments will never sway God in the slightest. God by no means alters His will to accommodate human desires or common sense. Instead, He looks for and delights in a faithful follower.

Are we trying to bargain with God offering Him justifications for our behavior? God doesn't negotiate that way. Partial obedience is disobedience in His eyes, and no sin is worth being outside His will! What is worse, the very people we are trying to impress with our foul mouths are the "sick" ones that need to hear Jesus coming from our mouth the most. What about respecting Jesus? If you wouldn't do it, if Jesus were standing next to you proves you know better.

Jesus Wants to Know, "Why Not?"

"Many will follow their shameful ways
and will bring the way of truth into dis-
repute." (2 Peter 2:2, NIV)

Knowing God is preparing judgment brings a sobering reality to Christians. Peter assures us that this is not speculation; it is inevitable and imminent.

With the one thing we know is for sure, "What kind of person should we be?" Many Christians attach great value to temporary stuff. I have acquaintances I feel like I need an appointment for them to put their phone down so we can carry on a conversation.

Possessions consume us, leaving little time or energy to invest in what is eternal. More than anyone else, Christians should be sensitive to the times in which we live.

We should walk so carefully with God that if He were preparing to bring judgment upon people, we would warn those in imminent peril.

Since Christ has been long-suffering, should we not invest our effort in building God's eternal kingdom? Jesus doesn't want to hear our justifications of why we are not talking and walking close to Him; He wants to know, "Why not?"

It Takes a Big Heart to Put Selfishness Aside

"So that your faith will not rest on men's wisdom, but on God's power." (1 Corinthians 2:5, NIV)

How big must God's heart be to save a small person like me? I mean, why would He see fit to bring me out of an eighteen-year addiction to meth? In response, how large has my heart grown to be? I can quickly tell, not by how I please the "important people," but by how I serve the ones society might deem lost from a relationship with their Savior, Jesus.

God chose the weak things of the earth to shame the strong so that no one can boast before Him. Yet I see some who brag about how often they go to their church, the numerous Bible study groups, and boast about what great Christians they are.

They have so much to be thankful to God, but they throw all that away by their actions and foul words around the people who need to see and hear Jesus in them the most. It takes a big heart to put your selfishness aside and to show compassion for the ones that are looking up to you. Never let your faith rest on your so-called wisdom, but on God's power.

What Will We Do When We Stand before Jesus?

"In fact, though by this time you ought
to be teachers, you need someone to teach
you the elementary truths of God's word
all over again." (Hebrews 5:12, NIV)

As a Christ-follower, we should all be on a continual growth and maturity level of righteousness. Though many people think those who know a lot about the Bible are the spiritually mature ones, Christian growth requires the discipline of godly habits carried out daily.

When our desire to obey the Lord is stronger than our attraction to sin, we'll know we are making progress in our spiritual life. Those who are mature in Christ recognize their inadequacy and rely on the Holy Spirit within them.

In God's eyes, maturity isn't the same as getting older. We can use our years to grow stronger in the Lord instead of wasting time being a "passive" Christian.

Spiritual growth requires a laborious pursuit of God. When we stand before Jesus one day to be accountable, how you going to feel telling your Savior, "Jesus, I wanted to be obedient to You, but I thought "fitting in" with those that needed Your Word the most was more critical." Right now would be the time to put your selfishness behind you and start living for Him.

A Sin Is a Sin, No Matter How Small

"Jesus replied, "I tell you the truth, everyone who sins is a slave to sin." (John 8:34, NIV)

True freedom is releasing from sin. Like a lie, no matter how small the lie is, it's still a lie. In Scripture, I notice when Jesus wants to drive something home, He will say, "I tell you the truth."

Some believe freedom is being able to act with few restraints, limits, or accountabilities. Even Christ-followers can find themselves in bondage to particular sins despite repeated attempts to change.

The Lord wants us to walk in freedom, and Jesus describes the pathway. Our faith in Christ should be the first step to help us stop even the smallest sins, including spewing filthy words from our mouth.

As we continue to read and meditate on Scripture, our minds, will, and emotions will be changed. Even the smallest of sins that once enticed us will become disgusting, and the emotional prisons will open as we discover our position in Christ. A sin is a sin, no matter how small. Isn't Jesus worth you being obedient to Him?

God Judges Righteously

> "But if you suffer for doing good and you endure it, this is commendable before God." (1 Peter 2:20, NIV)

The Bible passage, which says to turn the other cheek, may confuse us. Are we to stand while someone beats us up emotionally? That's not the message Jesus was delivering.

Pride will undoubtedly trigger a desire for revenge if a family member or co-worker repeatedly says unkind words. We may need to ignore the other person's actions, walk away from the abuse, or confront your enemy. Instead of trying to get even, we should seek to understand that person.

When they put you down and mistreat you, remember there is something wrong with them, not you. God's lesson for us to learn is when we endure unjust treatment, we are following in Christ's footsteps.

No one was treated more unjustly than the sinless Son of God. Yet He "did not revile in return" and "uttered no threats" but kept entrusting Himself to His Father, knowing that He judges righteously. God can handle our grievances if we respond as Christ did.

Our Old Life Was Self-Centered

"This righteousness from God comes through faith in Jesus Christ to all who believe." (Romans 3:22, NIV)

After placing trust in Jesus, a person should begin to walk in a new direction. Now that we are one with Jesus Christ, our mind renewed, and our behavior should become increasingly God-pleasing.

As God's children, we're also to saunter. That is, leaving an imprint and an influence wherever we go. When we take our pride and self-centeredness away and understand who we are in Christ, we begin to reflect the Lord Jesus to others.

The joy we have in Him becomes an expression of His presence in our lives and our relationship with Him. So think of the people we cross paths with each day. We might be reflecting Jesus to some who have been blind to the truth of God. We have no idea how many lives might be touched by ours.

Being called a leader is more than a title. It means our life must change so that everybody who meets us will meet Christ in us. Our old life was self-centered; our new life is Christ-centered.

Is that becoming more evident in you? How would Jesus react to a recording on your day? Let it reflect Jesus in all you say and do.

Take Time to Look Past Your Actions

"All a man's ways seem innocent to him,
but motives are weighed by the Lord."
(Proverbs 16:2, NIV)

How quick we are to question the motives of others, yet we are so slow to ask our own? I see some who, when guilty, excuse their offenses, concluding others are far too sensitive.

Regardless of how we monitor our motives, God weighs them in His scales of righteousness. It is useless to try to deceive God with our constant, self-centered justifications, for He sees our hearts.

Is it possible to do the right things for the wrong reasons? Of course, especially if your actions come from unhealthy motives such as pride, insecurity, ambition, lust, greed, guilt, anger, fear, and hurt. Yes, it is possible to do the best things based on the worst motives.

When the Lord measures our purposes, He looks for one thing: love. All that we do should proceed from our love for God and others. Take time to look past our actions to what lies behind them. Ask God to show us what He sees when He examines our motives.

Only God Can Resurrect What Is Lost

"Lord, I have heard of your fame; I
stand in awe of your deeds, O Lord."
(Habakkuk 3:2, NIV)

If you find that your heart has grown cold to God, that
the spiritual life of your family has waned, call out to God to
revive you.

Only God can restore life to something that has died. It
is not our activity, but our relationship with God that brings
experience. Over time, busyness creeps in, and we let sin
go unchallenged, or we take our relationship with God for
granted and not notice the gradual decline until we find ourselves drained of spiritual vitality.

At a time like this, it is futile to try to bring back life
yourself. We can organize many activities and encourage others around us, but only God can resurrect what is dead. If we
sense that the spiritual vigor has gone out of our life, or family, this is God's invitation to pray. He wants you to intercede
with Him so that He might revive His work. "I stand in awe
of your deeds, O Lord,"

"For the Son of Man is going to come in his Father's glory with his angels, and then he will reward each person according to what he has done." (Matthew 16:24, NIV)

Did you know we are held under a microscope because we call ourselves Christians? The Lord wants us to follow His instructions precisely. However, we like to add some of our desires and preferences to His plan.

Unfortunately, our human nature wants to pick and choose which parts of the Bible we will obey. A lifestyle of obedience requires commitment and perseverance. Our Savior calls all of us, yes, you too, that we should deny our selfish desires, live sacrificially, and follow Him.

So, Jesus wants to know; Is Jesus worth leading a godly life to bring honor and point others to Him? Knowing Jesus is coming soon, how will our reward be according to what we have done? "Father, we are all sinners, but today, would you open the eyes of those who are blind to what You call sin. Amen.

Some People See Us as the Only Bible They Read

"I will exalt you, my God the King; I will praise your name forever and ever."
(Psalm 145:1, NIV)

"Gratitude": the state of being grateful. There is another way to express gratefulness by serving God. Ultimately, we show the Lord our gratitude through obedience.

A holy life flows from a heart filled with thankfulness for God's grace, mercy, love, and salvation. What if today instead of living for ourselves and our pleasures, we wanted to exalt Christ in all that we do, say, and think? And as we allow God's Spirit to control us, He will faithfully enable us to live in a manner that is pleasing and honoring to the Lord.

We have to realize there are people all around us who see us as the only Bible they read. Is your gratitude toward the Lord enough to make you live in a manner that honors Him? You cannot tolerate sin in your life, expecting to receive His guidance in another.

Jesus Gave Us the Ultimate Sacrifice

"The one who sows to please his sinful nature, from that nature will reap destruction." (Galatians 6:8, NIV)

Working toward something without immediate results can be disheartening. However, some rewards aren't always instantly visible.

Doing good isn't the way to gain salvation, and Scripture doesn't specify whether what we reap will be now or in heaven. We can know there will be "a harvest of blessing." It's easy to feel that the good things we do are useless, like guarding our mouths or helping a stranger, but Paul explains, "a man will reap what he sows."

Our Savior, Jesus, gave us the ultimate sacrifice, dying a brutal death on the cross, all while you were on His mind. To me, because of His sacrifice, there are no excuses or justifications worth not gaining the harvest God wants us all to redeem one day.

Not all rewards are immediate or visible, so ask God to help you trust Him to be faithful in what He's called you to do. "Father, I pray for the problems we all have, but I want to pray for the one person reading this who has the tremendous problem of thinking they have no problems at all." Amen

Fellow Man Does Not Hold the
Keys to Your Salvation

"For my thoughts are not your thoughts,
neither are your ways my ways," declares
the Lord." (Isaiah 55:8, NIV)

I believe the Lord looks at each of us as a slab of granite, and He is the Master Sculptor. He lovingly wants to chip away everything that does not fit the masterpiece He is creating.

He chips away everything that does not match the image of His Son, like pride and selfishness. "That's just who I am, or I am not perfect," you say? When anything, anybody, or justifications become more important to us than the Lord, it is an idol in our life.

God's chisel hurts sometimes and feels as if the Lord is taking away everything we hold dear. Unless you understand His goal and believe He's working for your good, you'll think He's cruel.

If you will stop making excuses why you can't be obedient and instead ask Jesus to chip away the bad that surrounds you like justifying your means, put your trust in the Great Sculptor, not in your fellow man. They do not hold the keys to your salvation.

A Deep Sense of Awe Is Essential

"Through love and faithfulness sin is atoned for; through the fear of the Lord a man avoids evil." (Proverbs 16:6, NIV)

The fear of the Lord is the most significant deterrent for sin. Those who perceive God as a gentle grandfather will treat their sin shallow. They will live their life on their terms rather than God's. But a righteous fear of holy God will dramatically affect the way a person lives.

The apostle Paul feared God and knew that one day, he would stand in judgment to give an account for everything he had done. If we feel like we have become complacent and comfortable with what God considers sin, we are completely isolated from God's holiness. A deep sense of awe is essential to knowing God, including knowing we are not His equals.

Yes, He has forgiven us, but we are still His creatures. He is God, and we are not. Father, today I pray for all the justifiers out there in this world, but especially the one who thinks they are exempt from knowing the fear and reverence toward You. Amen.

There Is a Limit to God's Mercy

"I do not understand what I do. For what
I want to do, I do not do, but what I hate
I do." (Romans 7:1,5 NIV)

Have you noticed that not all Christians think the same way? Like the verse above, they use this as their anthem why they continue to sin.

In actuality, God was telling us that when we put on the Holy Spirit, the old self is gone, and the new person is put on. Picking and choosing a verse to justify something is not how God's grace and mercy works.

If you go forward in the same chapter, verse 25, "Thanks be to God, who delivers me through Jesus Christ our Lord!" There is a limit to God's mercy because it cannot contradict His other attributes—like holiness, righteousness, and justice.

Sin is punished for God to remain. These folks abuse God's abundant mercy by engaging in deliberate sin while telling themselves, "He forgives me." Shouldn't we be one who is redeemed and given eternal life to be overwhelmed with love and gratitude for what Christ did?

Never continue on your merry way, oblivious to the fact that justice, not mercy, awaits you in eternity. When are you going to start giving thanks to God, who delivers you through Jesus Christ, our Lord? Isn't that enough?

God Loves You because of Who God Is

"Rise up, O God, and defend your cause; remember how fools mock you all day long." (Psalm 74:22, NIV)

Our view of God is the most vital aspect of our life. The way we see the Lord determines what we believe about Him and how we think, act, and react in every situation.

Nothing in man deserves God's kindness, and how you respond to adversities speaks volumes about us. We can either blame God or bless Him. God hopes we choose Him so we would allow Him to work in our lives, to enlarge and, where necessary, correct our perception of Him.

God loves us because that's Who God is. The more we recognize His consideration for His creation, the deeper our faith and sense of peace will become.

Isn't it time we start defending God's cause? "Remember, how fools mock Him all day long." Not only is Jesus counting on us, but so is a fallen world who are watching and listening to our every word.

Acquiring Wisdom Takes Commitment

"Wisdom will save you from the ways of wicked men, from men whose words are perverse." (Proverbs 2:12, NIV)

No one wants to be a fool in God's eyes, but when someone justifies about the sins they partake in is doing thus ignoring, and living the way they want is playing the fool's game. That's telling Jesus, "I know you died a brutal death on the cross, but because of my self-reliance, I can justify why my ways are a substitute for godly judgment."

As we devote our attention to learning to know God, we'll understand what He desires and what He hates. If we diligently obey God's Word, wisdom will enter our hearts, guard our foul mouths, and protect us from evil deception to justify our means. We say, "I want to acquire more wisdom from the Lord," but are we willing to do what is required to receive it?

Acquiring wisdom takes commitment, diligence, and a single-minded pursuit, but the sacrifice for the One who hung on that cross is worth it. Never let the unfaithfulness of others determine what we do. Our obedience to Jesus far exceeds what others around us do. Don't get caught up in their trap.

What Kind of Home Are You Building for the Kingdom?

A great and wise man once called one of his contractor friends, saying, "Go out on my land and build a house for me. I will leave all the planning and construction to you, but remember, I want your work to be the very best you can do because it is for an exceptional friend of mine."

The contractor left feeling great that his friend trusted him that much. All kinds of building materials were available there, but the contractor had a mind of his own. "Surely," he thought, "I know my business. I can use a few inferior materials here and cheat on my artistry a little there, and still make the finished work look good, and I will be the only one who knows what I have built with the inferior materials and shoddy quality."

And so, at last, the work was completed, and the contractor reported back to the great and wise man. "Very good," the great and wise man said. "Now remember that I wanted you to use only the finest materials and craftsmanship in this house because I wanted to make it a present for an exceptional friend of mine? You are that person. It is all yours!"

How much like a man. He comes to earth a stranger. He has his free will. He may build as he likes. But on the morning of his resurrection, he will receive what he has created for an eternal home and habitation. What kind of home are you building for the kingdom?

Where Is Your Compass Pointing?

"He will bring glory to me by taking what is mine and making it known to you." (John 16:14, NIV)

When I am blessed to give my testimony, there is a part in it that reads, "Who we associate with is like a compass. It points to who we are associating with, and a compass never lies!"

Sin does to our understanding of the Lord's clear direction what a magnet does to the needle of a compass. In the same way, sin will mislead us.

Yielding to the Lord is an essential part of receiving His direction. We cannot tolerate sin in our lives and expect to receive His guidance in another.

So here is a simple test to ask ourselves when a decision is unclear. "Is Christ glorified in this choice, and can I do this in Jesus's name?" If either answer is no, don't follow that path, because the Holy Spirit is not guiding us there. His leading always aligns with Scripture and brings glory to God.

Jesus's View of Death

> I wanted to share perhaps what Jesus's
> view of death might be. "Precious in the
> sight of the Lord is the death of his saints"
> (Psalm 116:15, NIV)

Why would the Lord see "precious" in the death of a loved one? When we consider what is precious to the Lord is not confined to earthly beings but from a heavenly view.

When a loved one passes and arrives in God's heaven, it's no surprise, because God was looking for their arrival. It was precious in His eyes. And think about this: Imagine the Father's joy when He welcomes His children home and sees the absolute ecstasy in being face to face with His Son.

When death comes for the follower of Christ, God opens His arms to welcome that person into His presence. Imagine the last time your loved one's eyes close here on earth, the next time they opened, they were looking into the face of God!

Through our tears, we can see how precious that is in God's eyes. To see Jesus will be heavens' greatest joy. What a glorious reunion it will be one day soon. To God, a sunset, on the one hand, is a sunrise in another.

What If You Found Out You Were Going to Die Tomorrow?

"Teach us to number our days aright, that we may gain a heart of wisdom." (Psalm 90:12, NIV)

What if we found out we were going to die tomorrow? Would we be more delightful, more loving, or more forgiving?

Here is a trustworthy guarantee: "One-hundred out of one-hundred reading this at this moment will die one day." Things like a fatal disease bring our mortality to the forefront instead of letting it hide in the recesses of our minds.

God never promises us one more second here on planet earth. We do, however, have an eternal home with God. Reading this Psalm should remind us all that our hope is not in a doctor's diagnosis, but in a God who is "from everlasting to everlasting."

It is going to be God's will, not ours. Death doesn't discriminate on how big our house is, how much money we make, how old we are, or how important we think we are. Knowing this, how will we spend the time God gave us on earth?. For me, I will strive to please our King Jesus.

God Has the Habit of Picking Up Nobodies

"You are witnesses of these things." (Luke 24:48, NIV)

Do we often think the power of the Holy Spirit is only available to pastors? The truth is this power is a gift to every person who is willing to serve God and to recognize we cannot work for God without the aid of His Holy Spirit.

We also must admit that we are sinners and ask for repentance. These things are necessary to maintain intimacy with God.

Maybe we are allowing deliberate sin to enter into our lives? When we acknowledge that, we are "short-circuiting" the power of the Holy Spirit to work in and through us.

Knowing we don't have to be a pastor to unleash the power of the Holy Spirit is very important. Jesus even used a couple of ole' rusty fishermen, a tax collector, and more to carry on His mighty Word. When we trust in God to provide the stamina for the work, He calls us to do, and He will clothe us in power.

Have you noticed how God has a habit of picking up nobodies and making them somebody? No pastor certificate required. "You are witnesses of these things."

Jesus Is Alive and Active

"Where, O death, is your victory? Where, O death, is your sting?" (1 Corinthians 15:55, NIV)

The original witnesses of Jesus's most astounding miracle, Christ's disciples, finally believed Jesus was alive, and everything changed. Those doubting and helpless men transformed into passionate preachers of Christianity.

We can have the same confidence considering what Christ's resurrection achieved, and then letting it be the foundation of all we think, say, and do. Jesus is alive and active, not only in heaven but in our lives. Jesus's death is not the end.

Instead, it is the beginning of life as God intended—free from sin and all its negative consequences. Jesus's resurrection guarantees that believers become resurrected as well, receiving new glorified bodies that are durable, perfect, and eternal. We will also have the joy of being reunited with our loved ones in Christ and seeing our Savior face-to-face.

When we understand what Jesus's resurrection accomplished, there will be no reason to let worldly sorrows and care drag us into hopelessness. How beautiful, how marvelous, is Your love, Jesus. He would have died for you even if you were the only person on earth.

Only One Good Friday Offers Eternal Salvation

> "But he was pierced for our transgressions, he was crushed for our iniquities; the punishment that brought us peace was upon him, and by his wounds, we are healed." (Isaiah 53:5, NIV)

Isaiah told us about our Savior's death hundreds of years into the future before it happened. And think of Jesus, looking out and seeing mother Mary, John, and others. They loved Jesus deeply, but there was no way they could understand His motivations on this Good Friday.

As much as they wanted to help Jesus, it was something He had to do alone. Then came the moment alone, when a beaten, bleeding Son of Man cried out, "My God, My God, why have you forsaken me?" At that very moment, Jesus took on all the sins of the world.

This very second would be a time to shed "self" and live as the Lord desires; thankful. If we truly follow Christ, our response can be nothing other than to fall on our face in profound gratitude.

Many take the forgiveness of their sins lightly. It cost God a terrible price to forgive us and make us righteous. Walk and talk in a manner worthy of the righteousness He has given us. Father, forgive us when we let the "unfaithfulness" of others determine how we act and speak. I am profoundly grateful you saved a wretch like me. Amen.

Do You Start Your Prayers Off with a Want?

"But as for me, it is good to be near God."
(Psalm 74:28, NIV)

I have had people tell me, "With all that has happened to me, I have lost faith in God." They add, "I don't think He is listening to my prayers any longer, either."

Sometimes, the Lord will put us through many trials to see if we will turn to Him for guidance. When we go to the Lord telling Him how it should or shouldn't be, then we are doing our will, not God's will.

Maybe God isn't answering a prayer you are asking because He can see more about our tomorrow than we can remember about all our yesterdays combined.

God is our friend and wants to hear about our concerns. Most folks are surprised when I convey to them, "I never start my prayers off with a "want," but instead, I always start my prayers thanking Him for this day and all the blessings He has bestowed on me.

When I go into my "wants," then I always end with, "If it is your will, Lord." God is God and doesn't need any help running this world. He has this all under control. When we draw near to God, we are sure to be on His side. Our intimacy with God is His highest priority for our lives, and also determines the impact of our lives.

Do You Demand God to Perform Miracles?

"For this God is our God forever; he will be our guide even to the end." (Psalm 48:14, NIV)

What if the only thing you heard from your best friend was negativity instead of some praise and encouragement? You wouldn't be so excited to be around them, would you?

I see people continually asking God for miracles, assuming that in every situation, God needs to do the spectacular. They presume, for example, that God wants to heal anyone who is sick or provide a miraculous escape from every difficulty they face.

Jesus condemned those who insisted that He perform miracles because He knew their hearts. They prefer the miracle over the Miracle Worker. God calls this idolatry, and He discouraged it by refusing to provide miracles on demand.

Sometimes the greatest act of faith is to not ask for a miracle, but instead, pray for God's will, not ours. Maybe it is time to trust God so totally that we can say, "But if not Lord, I will still trust You."

That thorn in our side, maybe God telling us, "When are you going to have a relationship with me by praising Me?" Start your prayer glorifying your Savior, and then thanking Him for all He has done in our life first. Just as you like encouraging words, so does our Savior, Jesus.

They Never Thought They Would See You Up Here

"Do you see a man wise in his own eyes?
There is more hope for a fool than for
him." (Proverbs 26:12, NIV)

A man arrived in heaven and was looking around with Jesus. "Wow," the man said. "I never expected to see all these sinners up here in heaven?" Isn't that a thief over there who went to prison? Can't believe a sinner like him would be up here. And look over there. Isn't that ole' Kim Barlow? Wasn't he on meth for many years? What is that sinner doing up here? God must have made a mistake!"

"And why is everyone so quiet, so somber? Please give me a clue."

"Hush, child," Jesus said. "They're all in shock. No one thought they'd see you here!"

Throughout Scripture, we see that salvation is a gift received from a personal relationship with Jesus Christ. It is not a result of good works; instead, a person saved will naturally produce good works. Do people see you living for Christ?

I Must Have Been a Mistake

I often ponder, and even remember asking my mother if I was a "mistake?" You see, I was born almost seven years apart from my three other brothers. Mother always was quick to tell me, "Kim, you were not a mistake." She would always add how much she loved me.

Looking back on my childhood, and for every mom out there, please hear this: One thing that I admire most and sticks in my mind as a child was my Mom & Dad getting four boys up on Sunday mornings, getting us dressed, and to church. What a task that must have been, but my parents both knew how important it was to instill the Lord in us. Had they not, my life would not have been the same.

Mother, I miss you terribly, but I get peace in knowing you are in heaven, and because you enjoyed life so much here on earth, I know you are enjoying paradise even more. I know you are breathing the pure sweet air, and enjoying all the beautiful things in heaven.

I love and miss my mother, but I wouldn't take one minute away from you, because I know when you got to see Jesus's face was the greatest gift of all. Save me a seat up there, and I will see you and Daddy soon.

Almost Gave Jesus up for Fifty Cents

"He ordered his angels to guard you wherever you go." (Psalm 91:11, NIV)

Several years ago, a preacher from out-of-state accepted a call to a church in a city new to him. Some weeks after he arrived, he had to ride the bus from his home to the downtown area due to repairs happening on his vehicle.

When he sat down in the bus seat, he discovered that the driver had accidentally given him a quarter too much change. As he considered what to do, he thought to himself, 'You'd better give the coin back. It would be wrong to keep it.' Then he thought, 'Oh, forget it, it's only a quarter. Who would worry about this little amount anyway? The bus company gets too much fare; they will never miss it. Accept it as a gift from God and keep quiet.'

When his stop came, he paused momentarily at the door, and then he handed the quarter to the driver and said, "Here, you gave me too much change." The driver, with a smile, replied, "Aren't you the new preacher in town?" Yes, he replied.

Well, I have been thinking a lot lately about going somewhere to worship. I just wanted to see what you would do if I gave you too much change. I'll see you at church on Sunday.

When the preacher stepped off of the bus, he grabbed the nearest light pole, held on, and said, "Oh God, I almost sold your Son for a quarter!"

Our lives are the only Bible some people will ever read. What an example of how much people watch us as Christians and will put us to the test. Always be on guard. You carry the name of Christ on your shoulders when you call yourself Christian.

God, Are You There?

Rick volunteers with prison ministries, and in his work, he has become friends with a pastor of a small church called "Almighty God Tabernacle."

On a Saturday night, the pastor was working after hours and decided to call his wife before he left for home. It was about 10:00 PM, but his wife didn't answer the phone. The pastor let it ring many times.

He thought it was odd that she didn't answer, but decided to wrap up a few things and try again. When he tried again, she responded right away. He asked her why she hadn't answered before, and she said that it hadn't rung at their house.

They brushed it off as a fluke and went on their merry ways.

The following Monday, the pastor received a call at the church office, which was the phone that he'd used that Saturday night. The man that he spoke with wanted to know why he'd called on Saturday night.

The pastor couldn't figure out what the guy was saying. Then the man said, "It rang and rang, but I didn't answer." The pastor remembered the mishap and apologized for disturbing him, explaining that he'd intended to call his wife.

The man said, "That's OK. You see, I was planning to commit suicide on Saturday night, but before I did, I prayed, *God, if you're there, and you don't want me to do this, give me a sign now.* At that point, my phone started to ring. I looked at the caller ID, and it said, "Almighty God." I just got the courage today to call back. God's timing is always perfect.

God Looks and Listens for Our Thanks

"Give thanks in all circumstances, for
this is God's will for you in Christ Jesus."
(1 Thessalonians 5:18, NIV)

True thankfulness comes to you when you look beyond
your blessings to the source of those blessings.

Do you consider that when you accepted Jesus into
your heart, you received powerful gifts like being forgiven,
saved from death, and adopted as God's children?

Luke 17:15–6 tells the story of the ten lepers that Jesus
healed. Those ten men rushed to tell the good news to those
they loved, but only one considered the Source of that blessing. Yes, only one stopped to thank and worship the One
who had given him back his life.

You, too, have been healed and made whole by the
Savior! Though you and I are sinners and don't deserve one
drop of our Savior's amazing grace, we, too, have been healed
and made whole by God's only Son Jesus!

Do you, like the nine lepers, rush off so quickly to glory
in your blessings without stopping to thank your Redeemer?
God looks and listens for our thanks. Isn't it time to saturate
your life with thanksgiving to God?

The Prisoner Is You

"For with the measure you use, it will be
measured to you." (Luke 6:38, NIV)

All of us have been told hurtful things in our lives.
Sometimes it has been by someone we loved.

Some of us can't shake the penetrating "sting" and are
unable to let it go. "Because that person hurt me," we cry out
as a simple matter of pride. The injustice grows ever stronger
into a monster that we should not allow.

When we are bitter, we become resentful when we refuse
to deal honestly with hurt feelings. Then the matter festers in
our hearts. A growing sense of irritation can spread through
our spirit like a nasty infection. While it silently destroys our
life, the person who hurt us remains utterly unaware of our
feelings.

Are we asking God for guidance in our prayers to help
us be the forgiver? It's not easy to forgive, but the one God is
trying to change is you.

God commanded us to be loving, forgiving people. If
we hold a grudge, that is no one else's problem. Decide to
release the offender in your mind. If we're keeping details
fresh in our thoughts, we're trapping ourselves in a cycle of
pain.

If you have been holding onto bitterness, pray for the
strength to forgive, and when you do, you will release a prisoner. That prisoner is you.

What Would It Sound Like if You Listened?

"Those who honor me I will honor, but
those who despise me will be disdained."
(1 Samuel 2:30, NIV)

My pastor's sermon stuck with me. He said, "What will
the preacher say at your funeral? God is not pleased if we
praise and revere Him at church, or with other Christians,
but not at our school, workplace, or neighborhood.

What would it look like if we could step back and hear a
recording of the words that came out of our mouths, or could
look at a video of your day? Would it honor God?

God expects us to praise Him completely, with our
words, with our actions, and with our life. Your actions rest
with you. If we honor Him, He will honor us.

Father, open our eyes to see that others are waiting for
us as Christians to break the rules. We lean on you to guide
us to honor you. Amen.

Prayer Isn't for God; It's for You

"I am the Lord your God, who teaches you what is best for you, who directs you in the way you should go." (Isaiah 48:17, NIV)

Why should we pray if God already knows all our needs? The simple answer is; prayer isn't for God, it's for us, and to build our faith in Him.

God always answers our prayers with, yes, no, or maybe, but He still hears our prayers. God never disappoints those who seek His will.

Do we command God to perform a miracle then argue that He came up short when they don't get an answer? Expecting God to perform a miracle is idolatry. That is praising the miracle instead of the Miracle Maker.

The best advice for a Christian is to fix our hope on the Lord Jesus Christ. Welcome whatever fits His will for our life, and turn away from all that does not. Our circumstances may shift and change, but Jesus never does. "I am the Lord your God, who teaches you what is best for you, who directs you in the way you should go." Are we standing in His way?

Don't Be Distracted by Satan's Lying Voice

"But God demonstrates his own love for
us in this: While we were still sinners,
Christ died for us." (Romans 5:8, NIV)

Are you the exception out of billions of people that
thinks you aren't significant enough to be singled out that
God loves you? Satan loves to use that same worn-out lie,
insisting we are too weak, sinful, or scarred to merit the
Lord's love.

Do you want positive proof that God thinks we are
unique? Ready? Jesus Christ died for us. Because of the
Father's love for you, He sent His Son to die a brutal death
on the cross, all the while you were on His mind.

None of us deserve the Father's care and protection,
but thankfully, deserving isn't the basis for His love. Don't be
distracted by Satan's lying voice, and miss the opportunities
and love God has for you, yes you. If you feel far from God,
remember, it isn't Him that's moved.

Use Jesus as Our Model

> "The voice of the Lord is powerful; the voice of the Lord is majestic." (Psalm 29:4, NIV)

Have you stopped to think, the same Lord who sat as King bringing judgment over the earth in Noah's day is the same King who reigns over our turbulent rebellious world today? All this is no surprise to Him.

Whether in Noah's day or our own, the message is the same: "The Lord sits as King forever." Are God's power and control a comfort to us or a matter of concern? Our answer depends on how much we know and trust Him.

As in any relationship, trust and intimacy grow with being familiar with Jesus's examples. In Revelation 22:20, "Yes, I am coming quickly" (NIV) tells us the Voice that brought all things into existence controls time, circumstances, and nature. It seems so small that He would only want us to have a relationship with Him by using His Son Jesus as a model.

Are You Drifting Away from God?

"See to it, brothers, that none of you
has a sinful, unbelieving heart that turns
away from God." (Hebrews 3:12, NIV)

Are you like a boat set out on a lazy river without oars? Do we find ourselves drifting a slow and sluggish glide away from good practices like obedience? There are consequences for slipping into uncharted, dangerous waters.

If we are a "drifter," God's warnings to us will be ignored. If a Christian continually justifies his wandering ways and denies sin, his conscience becomes numbed, thus paving the way for more sinful behavior with less guilt.

As a drifting believer's conscience becomes numb, his spiritual ears are deaf. Truth cannot gain entrance because he has invited the wrong attitudes and philosophies into his thinking process.

People justify and drift from God in search of more, more freedom, choices, and pleasure. But the consequences of floating down that slow river of disobedience, is they end up with less.

If we feel like we are drifting, we are sacrificing the victorious life Christ so wants for us.

Who Is Your Pilot?

"He said to his disciples, "Why are you so afraid? Do you still have no faith?" (Mark 4:40, NIV)

A comfortable plane ride was about to get bumpy. The voice of the captain interrupted the in-flight beverage service and urged passengers to fasten their seat belts tightly.

Soon the plane began to roll and pitch like a ship on a wind-whipped ocean. While the rest of the passengers were doing their best to deal with the turbulence, a little girl sat through it all calmly, reading her book.

After the plane landed, a fellow passenger asked how she had been able to be so calm?

She responded, "It's easy! My daddy is the pilot, and he's taking me home."

What do you do when the ride gets a little bumpy? Our heavenly Father is the pilot, and He will guide us home safely. Put your trust in Him. Faith is not the absence of fear, but the willingness to go on when fear is present.

Jesus Protected His Own Time with the Father

"After he had dismissed them, he went
up on a mountainside by himself to pray.
When evening came, he was there alone."
(Matthew 14:23, NIV)

"Jesus, I'll catch up with you later. I am just way to busy right now." Sound familiar? What we fail to realize is that our quiet time with God is what empowers us to face the challenges of the day.

The busier our day, the more time we should spend praying for it all. Jesus protected His own time with the Father. I can't begin to think of any person having more on His mind, having more things to do, or being in higher demand than Jesus?

When Jesus was the busiest, were the times He pulled away from the crowds to pray. If Jesus considered prayer necessary to prepare for His most active days, shouldn't our busy time be an absolute essential for us to pray too?.

Father, we all have problems, but today, I pray for that one person that believes they have no problems at all.

Are Your Ambitions Selfish?

"My tongue will speak of your righteousness and of all your praises all day long."
(Psalm 35:28, NIV)

Some look at righteousness as something only Jesus can be. But Jesus wants us to pursue walking in His footsteps. There is no greater reward in our life than devoting ourselves to the pursuit of righteousness.

Jesus wants us to reflect the holiness of God that is ours by salvation, molding our thoughts, so nothing we think about would be inappropriate for a child of God. We must invite the Holy Spirit to work in our lives to help us with righteousness.

Jesus said if we seek first God and His justice, everything else will follow. If we want to harvest righteousness in our life tomorrow, we must plant seeds of goodness and obedience today.

So I ask you? What do people see or hear from you? Jesus wants us to reflect Him in all we do and say. What selfish ambition is keeping you from righteousness?

God's Word Is an Acquired Taste

"Like newborn babies, crave pure spiritual milk, so that by it you may grow up
in your salvation." (1 Peter 2:2, NIV)

I feel blessed on Sundays, getting to hear Jesus spoken where I attend church. It pumps me up to the point I walk out thinking, *Man those were right words! I can't wait until next week!*

Have you noticed right after someone has come to the Lord; their hunger for more of Him is evident? But as time passes, the novelty wears off, the problems of the day, and life's pressures continue as they did previously?

God's Word is an acquired taste, and the more we consume it, the higher our hunger for it will become. As you become more familiar with Scripture, you'll notice your desire and understanding for it increases.

Best of all, your love and devotion to your Savior will grow as well. Is your hunger for the Lord evident? If not, ask the Lord to restore your appetite, and you will crave that pure spiritual milk.

No One Is More Precious in the Lord's Sight

> "If anyone acknowledges that Jesus is the Son of God, God lives in him and he in God." (1 John 4:15, NIV)

It is mind-boggling to be set apart by God, knowing that God observes your sacred life and is pleased with what He sees.

What an immense privilege to know your life holds a special place in God's heart. You may feel like you are one person in this big world we live in, but to God, you are one extraordinary person to Him.

I see award shows and other accolades always trying to find new ways to honor people, but even the world's most extravagant awards are worthless compared to the immeasurable blessing of holding a special place in the heart of God.

No one is more precious in the Lord's sight than when He finds someone who strives to live a righteous life and bring glory to Him.

Let us spend more time glorifying our precious Savior today and always. I am Kim Barlow, I love Jesus, and I approve of this message.

We Cannot Earn Jesus Christ's Love

"Dear friend, do not imitate what is evil
but what is good." (3 John 1:11, NIV)

The night before His crucifixion, Jesus was praying at Gethsemane when Judas Iscariot approached Him with a band of men and then reached out to kiss Jesus.

Today the man's name is synonymous with those who betray others for personal gain. In spite of Judas's greed and betrayal, Jesus never stopped loving him, still using the word "friend" to address the disciple.

The Lord does not place conditions on His love. We cannot earn Jesus Christ's love and friendship. So I submit to you today all of us sinners. (Yes, that includes you and me.) Jesus reaches out and draws us into fellowship those who are willing.

Not one of us sinners are worthy but are privileged to live in His love anyway. With this, why oh why would you not let people see and hear Jesus coming from you? For me, you not giving Jesus 100 percent is telling Him you would rather imitate what is evil instead of what is right.

Beware of people who brag about who they are in Christ A lion never has to tell anyone who he is!

Today Is a Brand-New Day

> He fell to the ground and heard a voice
> say to him, "Saul, Saul, why do you per-
> secute me?" (Acts 9:4, NIV)

I love how Jesus picked some pretty rough and tough characters to become His disciples.

In Acts 9, Ananias saw Saul the Pharisee, who was having people persecuted and executed. But God told Ananias not to focus on who Saul was but to focus on who he had become.

If you are like me, we sometimes see ourselves only as who we were with all our failures and disobedience, but God sees us as new creations, and who we are becoming through the power of the Holy Spirit.

If you are looking and living for your past, it is time you forgave yourself! God certainly has and wants you to become an instrument to whom others wish to what you have, namely Jesus Christ in you!

Today is a brand new day to ask the Lord to help you have a better view of yourself. Heck, if Jesus can save a former meth-head and sinner like me, He certainly will love you too! Are you in for Jesus?

God Gave Us Our First Breath

"In his hand is the life of every creature and the *breath* of all mankind." (Job 12:10, NIV)

A man arrived in heaven. St. Peter was showing him around, when the man said, "St. Peter, could I ask you a question?" St. Peter said, "Yes." The man asked, "Why didn't God ever send someone to cure cancer and all the other diseases that killed so many people while I was on earth?"

St. Peter, with a shocked look on his face, answered, "Are you kidding me? God sent someone to cure those horrible diseases many times, but you folks kept aborting them!"

I am sorry, but if it has a heartbeat, then only God gave it life, and no one can take that from His creation, period.

Only God gave you your first breath, and He will take your last one from you.

There is an abortion in the United States every twenty-five seconds, and every twenty-five seconds that clicks by, add one more. I am sure some will try and justify this, but I will leave it up to God to sort it out one day, as we will all have to be accountable to Him. Father, please forgive us

You Don't Have to Be a Pastor to Speak of Jesus

"You are witnesses of these things." (Luke 24:48, NIV)

Do you often think the power of the Holy Spirit is only available to pastors? The truth is the power of the Holy Spirit is available to every person who is willing to serve God. We have to recognize we cannot work for God without the aid of His Holy Spirit.

We also must admit that we are sinners and ask for repentance. These things are necessary to maintain intimacy with God.

Maybe you are allowing deliberate sin to enter into your life? If we allow that, we are "short-circuiting" the power of the Holy Spirit to work in and through us. Knowing we don't have to be a pastor to unleash the power of the Holy Spirit is very important.

Jesus even used a couple of ole' rusty fishermen, a tax collector, and more to carry on His mighty Word. When we trust in God to provide the stamina for the work He calls us to do, then we're covered in His power.

Have you noticed how God has a habit of picking up nobodies and making them somebody?

No pastor certificate required. "You are witnesses of these things," and doing so, everyone you meet will see Jesus in you.

Praying in His Will, Not Our Will

"Your kingdom come, your will be done on earth as it is in heaven." (Matthew 6:10, NIV)

Your relationship with God ought to bring you more pleasure and joy than any other activity, connection, or material possession. So how do we find comfort in what God enjoys?

Only as we spend intimate time with Him will we begin to take delight in the things God loves. As you adjust to yourself to God, your heart will start to desire the same things God's heart desires. Your first request in prayer will not be for yourself, but for God's name to be exalted.

Have you been asking God to give you the desires of your heart without first seeking to understand what's on His heart? God places this critical requirement for those who pray: that we find His priorities and make them our own. This vital requirement prevents us from asking out of selfishness. As for me, I will always ask for my prayers to be God's will, not mine.

Are You the Director of Your Life?

"For you created my inmost being; you knit me in my mother's womb." (Psalm 139:13, NIV)

Do you feel as if God's plan for you has jumped the track?

Your heavenly Father teaches you even before you were born; God predetermined what He wanted to accomplish in, through, and for you.

His wisdom, He directs events and chooses the precise timing to help you grow as a Christian. His love motivates everything He does in your life to make you more like His Son.

From a human perspective, God's plan for you may seem too slow or too hard to follow. It does not have to be this way.

With the help of the Holy Spirit, you can hold fast during those periods when you want to direct your own life.

Your path may seem dark to you, but in His light, the way becomes clear. All you have to do is follow.

Teach Us How to Love the Unloveable

"Dear friends, since God so loved us, we ought to love one another." (1 John 4:11, NIV)

What a hard pill to swallow when there is someone in your life you're struggling to love.

Is there someone in your life, despite your good intentions, efforts, it seems impossible to muster love and affection toward them?

You know you should love everyone, but that doesn't automatically make you adequate for the task. Although the Lord has richly poured His love into our hearts, you have the responsibility to grow in it.

As you submit to Christ's life, people will notice Christ in you through selfless, sacrificial care for others. Every unlovable person in your life is an opportunity to let God teach you, love.

Becoming more intimate through God's Word will make your adoration of Him increase, and teach you how to love the ones you are struggling to love.

Father, teach us to love even the ones we find hard to love. You so loved us; we ought to love one another.

Never Become Satisfied with Religious Activity

> "What is more, I consider everything a loss compared to the surpassing greatness of knowing Christ Jesus my Lord, for whose sake I have lost all things."
> (Philippians 3:8, NIV)

Bible study groups, serving in the church, doing good deeds, or reading Christian books, won't give you eternal life.

In Jesus's day, the Pharisees loved to recite God's law for hours on end. Yet Jesus condemned them because, although they knew the Scriptures, they did not know God. It was a cunning temptation to prefer the book instead of the author.

No amount of Christian activity will ever replace your relationship with Jesus. The Apostle Paul considered every "good" thing he had ever done to be "rubbish" when compared to the surpassing value of knowing Christ.

Never become satisfied with religious activity rather than a personal, deep, and growing relationship with Jesus Christ.

When writing the story of your life, never let someone else hold the pen.

What Is Distracting You from Knowing the Lord?

> "Love the Lord your God with all your
> heart and with all your soul and with all
> your mind and with all your strength."
> (Mark 12:30, NIV)

In any relationship, love develops as you learn to know and appreciate the other person. Knowing God requires a starting place.

The problem exists when our souls are often self-absorbed, and our minds are easily distracted. Because we reside on planet earth, it demands your time, attention, and energy. All these can make you fail to focus on the One who is worthy of every minute of your devotion.

What is distracting you from seeking to know and love the Lord? Start today to carve out a time to let the Lord speak to you through His Word while talking to Him in prayer. To know Him is to love Him, and by doing this, you will discover your amazing God and His Son Jesus Christ.

Obedience Is a Vast Word

"If I had not come and spoken to them, they would not be guilty of sin. Now, however, they have no excuse for their sin." (John 15:22, NIV)

What does your lifestyle reveal about the depth of your devotion to Christ? Do others see it clearly in the words you speak, your conduct, or your character?

By His obedience Love for His heavenly Father, Jesus's love was perfectly demonstrated. The word obedience is a huge word, but if you look at the intimate relationship Jesus had with the Father, you would understand why Jesus was delighted to honor and obey Him.

If you feel that your love for Christ seems small, open the Word of God, and obey whatever He says. He will remain with you and disclose Himself, which will increase your capacity to love and know Him more. Until you're willing to let go of what's not right for you, you can't have what is.

No One Can Hinder God

"What I have said, that will I bring about; what I have planned, that will I do." (Isaiah 46:11, NIV)

Sometimes, I feel people around me try to cancel God's will for me. If you feel like that, here's the excellent news. The decisions and disobedience of others will not nullify God's will for you.

Other people's actions will affect you, but no one can prevent what God wants to do in and through you. Maybe you felt that someone bullies or ridicules you, thus trying to thwart God's will for you? Mere man cannot stop God from accomplishing His purposes in your life! Once God sets something in motion, no one can stop it.

Father, teach each of us to use your Son Jesus as our model when we speak. Let us think before we speak and to ask Jesus; How should I say this, my Lord? Protect those who feel from their insecurities believe they need to bully or ridicule others to make themselves look better. Amen.

Are You Longing for Assurance?

"For this reason I kneel before the Father."
(Ephesians 3:14, NIV)

Being a Christian doesn't automatically make you feel complete. During my 18-year addiction to meth, in theory, I knew that the Lord loved me, but I didn't feel it.

Only after the Lord spoke to me one early morning during my addiction, did He allow me to take an in-depth look into my fractured soul to experience His love in a personal way. Once I felt the security of Jesus's love for me, I knew with Him; I could walk in His will and kick that addiction behind me in His name.

Maybe you are longing for fullness to have the ability to have a one-on-one relationship with Jesus Christ? A relationship like this is possible only if you are willing to open up and let the Lord search your heart. In this way, Jesus will reveal to you what's holding you back from accepting His love.

Do You Exercise Your Faith Muscles?

"Now faith is being sure of what we hope
for and certain of what we do not see."
(Hebrews 11:1, NIV)

Have you ever said, "I wish I had great faith." Faith is like working a muscle. You must exercise it to keep it active. Wishing won't cut it.

As a Christian, you are to believe God not only for redemption but for everything in your life. Weak faith hopes that God will do as He says, but strong faith knows He is faithful to accomplish all He says He will do.

You may be thinking, *I am not good enough for the Father to use me*, but the Bible has many examples of flawed people whom the Lord used to fulfill His purposes.

He isn't looking for perfection but, rather, individuals willing to believe in Him. He doesn't merely work through people of faith; He transforms them.

Start by reading God's Word to learn what He wants you to do. Trust Him and do what He says—your faith muscles will grow, and He will have the glory. Opening your Bible in a quiet place will be the best exercise you have ever had.

My Business Card Would Read *Sinner*

"Here is a trustworthy saying that deserves full acceptance: Christ Jesus came into the world to save sinners—of whom I am the worst." (1 Timothy 1:15, NIV)

If I had a business card title below my name, it would read: "Sinner." I have observed that most folks don't like to consider themselves a sinner.

If Paul had a title below his name, it would read: "Apostle." But in Paul's past, his card title would have read: "Blasphemer, Persecutor, and Murderer." Jesus picked some pretty rough folks to carry out what He had planned. But because of God's mercy, Paul was now called, "Apostle," one to whom Jesus sent out to share the glorious news of the gospel.

What is even more amazing is like the apostle Paul, we are sent out by the King of Kings to the world. Jesus wants a sinner like me and you to fulfill His gospel to the world. With humility, I pray you to recognize none of us deserve such a commission either. It is our privilege to represent Him to the world in word and deed to all around us.

How High on the Totem Pole, Are You?

"If anyone would come after me, he must
deny himself and take up his cross daily
and follow me." (Luke 9:23, NIV)

Humility: "freedom from pride or arrogance: the quality or state of being humble."

You will never see an award for first place for humility; instead, our culture awards high achievement, external beauty, or how high on the totem pole you are.

If you choose God's way of humility, He promises spiritual blessings will follow. Too many times, in our arrogant self-sufficiency, God will oppose us because you are working against Him.

God will become your source of confidence and strength, but only when you humble yourself too yield to His authority and then obey Him.

This society awards us on instant gratification for achievements, but God honors you according to His perfect ways and timing.

Will you humble yourself and live for God's glory rather than your own, or will you continue to plot your course inviting His opposition?

God Has so Much in Store for Us.

> "Now to him who is able to do immeasurably more than all we ask or imagine, according to his power that is work within us." (Ephesians 3:20, NIV)

The most exciting times in our life will come from God's actions, not ours. The people God uses mightly in Scripture were ordinary people whom God gave divine assignments that they could never have initiated.

Jesus selected the twelve disciples, all regular, uneducated men, when He was ready to take the good news of His salvation to the world. Through the ages, God has chosen the everyday lives of people to accomplish things through them that they could never have imagined.

I experienced God initiating something new in my life when He spoke to me one early morning while locked in my eighteen-year addiction to meth, talking to me, *this was over, and He was going to take me out of it!* And that's what He did, with no rehab!

When the Lord tells you what His plans are, trust Him, and walk carefully with Him. God has so much in store for us all if you will not let the busyness of your life get in the way. God will accomplish things through your life that you never dreamed possible.

God certainly touched this ole' wretch, and He can reach you too! Never give up hope because the Lord just might be trying to surprise you also. Thank you, sweet Jesus, for saving a sinner and wretch like me! Amazing grace. Amen.

Where Do Sinners Go?

"God also said to Moses, "I am the Lord.""
(Exodus 6:2, NIV)

As God has walked with His people through the generations, He has revealed Himself as to the needs of His people.

And what about you? Has God tried to reveal His character to you according to your needs and His purposes? As you obey Him, it will naturally make you understand Him. When you face a severe obstacle, He will unveil that He is God Almighty.

Our understanding of God's character and our knowledge of Him ought to be much higher today than when we first became Christian. Sadly, some Christians continue to live year after year with the same essential awareness of God that they had when they first began walking with Him.

I bet someone is reading this right now thinking, *I don't have to go to church to be a Christian!* Well, maybe not, but if you got married and never went home, how strong is that relationship going to be?

Whatever your present situation, see it in the light of what God is teaching you, through circumstances, about Himself, and you will come to know God in ways you have never know Him before. He is waiting to whisper to you, "I am the Lord." Are you listening?

Walk Humbly with the Lord

"The man said, "The woman you put here with me—she gave me some fruit from the tree, and I ate it." (Genesis 3:12, NIV)

Ahhh, the "blame game." It has been around since the beginning of man, and sadly though, even as adults, many people still play the blame game.

Maybe we do it thinking we can avoid undesirable consequences, or how about a chance to make us look more favorably to others? Sometimes, it isn't other's we blame, but circumstances. *The way I was treated, or that's how I was brought up*, we say.

Regardless of the justifications, sin is never justifiable, and God always holds us accountable. While it seems complicated for some to swallow their pride and admit they are wrong, it's still best to take full responsibility for your attitudes, responses, and behavior.

That is the only way to walk humbly with the Lord, which pleases and honors Him. No one wins by shifting blame and refusing to take responsibility.

Father, please open our eyes and hearts and teach us that the "blame game" is the easy way out. Admitting our faults to You, and swallowing our pride, will always honor You. Amen.

Are We Too Busy Finding Ourselves?

> "But land that produces thorns and this-
> tles is worthless and is in danger of being
> cursed. In the end, it will be burned."
> (Hebrews 6:8, NIV)

In this fast-paced society today, waiting has become a lost art. But God's character qualities He values take time to develop. Could there be anything more valuable or important in life than to have the capacity to know the mind of God?

We can learn His mind right now by simply opening His Owners Manual to read His Word in Scripture. We might be so busy finding ourselves trying to figure out God's will and His direction that we fail to hear His voice.

Our challenge for today and every day is to make it a priority to spend some quiet time with the Lord in His Word. It will be worth the effort, even if it means rearranging our schedule. Wisdom awaits us if we read the mind of God through the God-breathed Scriptures.

Every Step of Faith Leads You to a Deeper Relationship

"Whoever can be trusted with very little can also be trusted with much." (Luke 16:10, NIV)

Throughout our life, God will seek to grow us in our faith. I can see this as I am plowing through writing my book. I see your eyebrows raise, and your faithlessness, but I am telling you this. Before I ever had any faith that I could write this book about my eighteen-year addiction to meth, I said, "no," but God said, "Yes, you can!"

How faithful have you been with what God has given you? If you have not been steadfast with the little God has given you, He will not trust you with more. God will not lead us beyond our present level of trust and obedience to Him. Instead, He will lead us to our area of unfaithfulness until we become prepared to trust Him.

We stand at an exciting new door of opportunity to know God more intimately every time we believe Him. Every step of faith leads us to a deeper relationship of trust with Him.

Are you passing up your open invitation to know God more intimately? Father, please teach us to have more faith in You.

Epilogue

As I bring my book to a close, I have some final thoughts. My clinging Scripture in the Bible for me has always been Psalm 91:11: "For he will command his angels concerning you to guard you in all your ways" (NIV).

Psalm 91:11 has so much meaning to me, for had it not been for the Lord sending angels to guard me, I would not be alive to write this book.

Maybe you got here feeling trapped in addiction or a situation you feel like there is no way out. I pray this story will help you realize that nothing is too big for God. If you fill your mind on things above, it will leave little room for the temptations of the evil one.

To think I thought meth was the most excellent *high* anyone could experience, but I can speak to you another *high* like non-other. It is the *high* you can experience with Jesus Christ!

I hope a closer relationship with Jesus Christ and the benefits that go with it will be one of your paths back toward Him.

Whenever the Lord gives you this righteousness, I pray you will think again and be able to authenticate God drew something useful from your suffering.

God has not forgotten you. God made you in His image. He never made any junk, including you.

His invitation is open to all to come running back to His arms. It is my prayer; you will claim it for yourselves. May the Lord richly bless you all the days of your life. Amen.

The end.

Printed in the USA
CPSIA information can be obtained
at www.ICGtesting.com
LVHW021402240524
780937LV00012B/617